"Through this delightful read, Mark Rosenberger introduces us to Dan, a newly appointed CEO, who finds all is not well with the company he has just joined. Mark cleverly draws the parallels between a high risk circus act and the prerequisites for a successful business based on the premise of how to be 'caught more and dropped less by the people you count on most.' Did Dan turn the company around? Did anyone fall from the trapeze? You will have to read this entertaining yet insightful book to find out."

Malcolm Franks — Director
CALIFORNIA COUNCIL FOR EXCELLENCE
Founding CEO
BRITISH QUALITY FOUNDATION

"Awesome book! I am very impressed with how Mark Rosenberger weaved Trapeze Buddy concepts from his personal values into a story. Mark is a wonderful author and *The Trapeze Buddy Success Strategy* will be a powerful tool for everyone who reads it."

Greg Cortopassi — Founder and CEO
TEAMWORKS TRAINING CORPORATION

"In *The Trapeze Buddy Success Strategy*, Mark Rosenberger has captured the true essence of business success in the 21st Century. His use of acronyms and metaphors will create a picture of success you can paint for your organization. I truly believe this manuscript offers the path to success regardless of your business or industry. And, it is a work easily applicable by anyone.

"Powerful, unique, useful. Here's the perfect model to be caught more and dropped less."

Ken Blanchard, coauthor
THE ONE MINUTE MANAGER®

"The trapeze buddy vision stays in your head after reading the book, more so than some others I've read."

Marsha Wilson, Executive Assistant
THE KEN BLANCHARD COMPANIES

"*The Trapeze Buddy Success Strategy* is a mental pick-me-up for increasing personal and professional results. Success in any endeavor is about relationships, and this book will show you how to develop strong relationships with the important people in your life that won't let you down."

Mark Sanborn, CSP, CPAE, Author
SANBORN & ASSOCIATES, INC.

"In an era when teamwork and mentoring are paramount to every organization's success, Mark Rosenberger's new book, *The Trapeze Buddy Success Strategy*, captures the how to's better than other books I've read. I strongly recommend it for every manager who wants to maximize company performance."

Tom Hinton — Author, Professional Speaker, CEO
CUSTOMER RELATIONS INSTITUTE

"An outstanding book, complete with a link to the strength of the human spirit!"
> *Jerry Fritz — Program Director for Sales and Customer Service*
> **EXECUTIVE EDUCATION IN THE SCHOOL OF BUSINESS, UNIVERSITY OF WISCONSIN-MADISON**

"*The Trapeze Buddy Success Strategy* hits the nail on the head. The concept brings home the valuable relationships we have in our lives. You can just visualize all the Splats! Going on all over the world everyday! I thoroughly enjoyed reading this book."
> *Jeanne Imbrogno — Manager of Customer Service*
> **GROUP 4 SECURITAS**

"*The Trapeze Buddy Success Strategy* is easy to read and really makes it simple to understand how the metaphor Trapeze Buddies can play an important role in building teamwork and trust in an organization."
> *Don Nelson — Area Manager*
> **CAGWIN & DORWARD**

"The Trapeze Buddy concept just makes sense. It helps create a language and company cultural which reinforces the need for every person to do their part. When we tell each other we're counting on one another to 'come through' it brings up a vivid mental image of either a caught or dropped business associate. Well done!"
> *Jack Simpson — Acting General Manager*
> **POTAWATOMI BINGO CASINO**

"Bravo! You did it! Your story line captures the essence of how to enhance teamwork, trust and support. I laughed, I took plenty of notes and I shared it with all my buddies!"

Cinda L. Daly — President
FOCUS INFORMATION SYSTEMS

"Teamwork is essential in the Fitness industry if we're going to create long-term success. The Trapeze Buddy Model is the best example I've seen of what it takes to work effectively as a team with the goal of impressing our members. It's common sense put into a story everyone will understand! Bravo! Way to go!"

George Jackson, Founder
E/GYM, INC.

"If Perspective influences behavior, and we know that it does, The Trapeze Buddy Success Strategy will become a classic as it helps take existing perspectives to a new level. Brilliantly presented."

Bob Googe, President; Author, Speaker
GEN-4, INC.

The Trapeze Buddy Success Strategy

by Mark Rosenberger

A New Way to Create Trust, Support and Teamwork in Your Business

The Trapeze Buddy Success Strategy:
A New Way to Create Trust, Support and Teamwork in Your Business
By Mark E. Rosenberger

www.trapezebuddy.com

Copyright 2002 by Mark E. Rosenberger. All rights reserved. No part of this book may be reproduced or transmitted in any form or by any means, electronic or mechanical, including photocopying, recording or by any information storage and retrieval system without written permission from the author, except for inclusion of brief quotations in a review.

Published by:
    WOW! Publishing
    10680 Loire Ave.
    San Diego, CA 92131 U.S.A.
    (858) 578-7900

Trapeze Buddy and Trapeze Buddies are trademarks of WOW! Performance Coaching, Inc.

Library of Congress Cataloging-in-Publication Data

Rosenberger, Mark E.
The Trapeze Buddy Success Strategy: A New Way to Create Trust, Support and Teamwork in Your Business/ Mark E. Rosenberger.
1st edition.

ISBN 0-9656567-1-3

Printed in the United States of America
First Printing: June 2002
10 9 8 7 6 5 4 3 2 1

Dedication

It's fascinating what a lakeside chat can produce. Trust vs. Fear. Believing in a dream and moving forward in an act of faith.

To all the Trapeze Buddies who everyday climb high, spin and reach for their partners. Every day is an act of faith.

To my favorite Trapeze Buddies at home—I am truly blessed!

The Trapeze Buddy Success Strategy

Contents

Introduction..13
Chapter 1: A Tough First Week..17
    You'll be able to relate!
Chapter 2: The Broken Boy...31
    We all have our challenges!
Chapter 3: Dropped Again...39
    Learning to move forward, despite…
Chapter 4: Being Caught Is A Whole
    Lot More Fun..51
    Applying in flight adjustments.
Chapter 5: Mind Mapping..63
    You have loads of Trapeze Buddies!
Chapter 6: C.A.T.C.H. Technology...................................71
    Success begins with C.A.T.C.H.
Chapter 7: The Trapeze Buddy
    Concept Revealed..85
    The Game: Be caught more and dropped less!
Chapter 8: The Trapeze Buddy
    Report Card..101
    We all have them, let's use them!
Chapter 9: Trapeze Buddy Distinctions........................115
    A clearer picture with distinctions!
Chapter 10: Success Characteristics...............................129
    What it takes to win from day one!
Chapter 11: Your First Big Step......................................143
    It's time to move forward!
Acknowledgements...155
About the Author..157

"Most of the important things in the world have been accomplished by people who have kept on trying when there seemed to be no hope at all."
– *Dale Carnegie*

Introduction

Let's face it—your business is not easy! Everyday you're counting on scores of people to make your life work and when they don't come through it can get pretty ugly.

Every week is filled with examples of people who didn't keep their word and you suffered the consequences of countless headaches and hassles.

That's why we've created this book. You'll discover through this simple, yet dynamically powerful metaphor—Trapeze Buddies™—how to be caught more and dropped less by the people you count on most!

As a result of reading this story, you'll end each day with:
- Fewer headaches and hassles
- More wins and fewer losses
- More fun, happiness, joy and peace-of-mind
- Trust, teamwork and personal responsibility
- Increased energy and focus

- Less stress
- An added bounce in your step

You know from experience that being dropped is no fun. The sound of "**SPLAT!**" is not music to your ears.

We've all been there.

>**Splat!**

Face down in the concrete.

>**Splat!**

Again.

>**Splat!**

One more time, people who said they'd come through did not. They either forgot, didn't care, said they would **try** to be there (I especially love this word—try), or did show up, but didn't have all the information, materials or know-how…and you're left hanging. Or, should I say, you're left falling.

Heading for earth. Preparing to hear that all too familiar sound, **SPLAT!**

And, in your business, there are no safety nets! In fact, there are usually spikes sticking out of the concrete, and one more time you come home with severe spike marks. Ouch!

Allow me to offer an important insight: you'll never reap the rewards of the positive benefits if you keep this story to yourself. You must share the concept and create your own team of high performing Trapeze Buddies!

Pass the story on to others. Spread the word. Share the book. Better yet, buy 10 copies for your most important Trapeze Buddies. Before you know it, the sound of "**SPLAT!**" will be just a dull memory from days gone by. (You may still have a slight nervous twitch from past SPLATS!, but we'll work you through those in due time.)

Please, have fun and consider:
How would you feel if you knew that the people you were counting on every day would never, ever let you down?

To Your Continued Success,
Mark Rosenberger
San Diego, CA

> "Only those who will risk going too far can possibly find out how far one can go."
> – *T.S. Eliot*

Chapter One
A Tough First Week

"Splat!" We've all been there before—someone you were counting on didn't come through as promised. Life gets pretty tough. It's filled with needless headaches and hassles. If only people would do what they said they'd do in the manner in which they said they'd do it. My job and life would be so much easier!

That's what Dan Branston, the new CEO of BoMar Industries, Ltd. was lamenting as he stood on the fourth floor of his office admiring a herd of North American elk in the gray mist below. He now understood why his Native American friends held the elk in such high regard, symbols of strength and stamina. Dan's office was situated on a farm like setting on the outskirts of town. From his fourth floor window he could observe the elk moving freely on the wildlife preserve established on the property by the founding owner. "They will be a constant reminder for me," thought Dan. "Strength and stamina will be key as we begin the process."

Contemplating his new assignment and the challenges which lay ahead, Dan knew that turning around a 40-year-old company would not be easy. A massive culture shift was needed to remain competitive in the ever-expanding global market.

BoMar Industries was not the first challenge Dan had undertaken as a "turn around specialist" CEO. He had made a name for himself as a go-getter with strong intuition. His expertise grew by helping teams discover new possibilities and thus transform the entire organization. Dan had been nicknamed "The Wizard" by his colleagues because of his ability to grasp the impossible.

But BoMar was a different challenge. After 40 years as an industry leader, BoMar had become complacent, slow and sluggish. Dan's intuition told him that something was missing, but he had yet to put his finger on the exact challenge.

The intercom interrupted his contemplative gaze at the elk.

"Mr. Branston, your staff meeting is in fifteen minutes. Is there anything else I can pull together for you?" asked his executive assistant, Nathalie James.

"Thank you, Nathalie. I'll just need a yellow pad and pen. And, of course, directions to the conference room."

"I'll be happy to walk the new guy down to the conference room. It wouldn't look good for you to get lost on your first day," Nathalie offered lightheartedly, but with the utmost respect.

Reputation indicated Nathalie was the perfect Executive Assistant—reliable, assertive but a bit on the outspoken side from time to time.

Dan quickly gathered his thoughts about the upcoming meeting. It was his first session with the Leadership Team. He'd been anticipating the chance to see how the "movers and shakers" of the organization perceived the company, the competition and the challenges.

"Ask questions, listen carefully," Dan reminded himself as he reviewed his notes, for he could sometimes be rather impatient. "There are GREAT ideas within this company; I just need to discover them."

It was a leadership style that had served him well in the past. He planned to use the strategy again today.

Nathalie promptly appeared at Dan's office door. "Ready when you are for your guided tour," she offered.

Meeting the Leadership Team...

Rich, dark and expensive best described the Executive conference room. It was clear no expense had been spared in the design and furnishing of the boardroom. Highly polished cherry wood cabinets and overstuffed leather conference chairs added to the rooms distinguishing character.

Dan exchanged greetings and handshakes with the Leadership Team then moved right into the purpose of the meeting. He wasn't curt but focused, deliberate and intentional; there was much to cover and accomplish in a short time span. Exactly the way Dan liked to operate.

Each of the seven leaders offered a quick review of his or her responsibilities and current projects. The comments were couched in a tone of egotistical platitudes. "Give the boss exactly what he wants to hear" seemed to be the theme of the meeting.

Unfortunately, the "them-against-us" mentality and the "happy stories" were the last thing the new CEO wanted to hear. He began tapping his pen impatiently on his yellow pad.

He had expected folks to be a bit guarded as they felt their way with "the new guy." He anticipated some rather vague answers and no real commitment to the challenges at hand. But this was crazy. Where were the "leaders" on the Leadership Team?

"This could be a more challenging project than I had imagined," commented Dan under his breath. He had just asked the group to share with him the values of the organization.

Silence.

Barb Moss, Head of Distribution, offered what appeared to be more of a guess than a statement: "Make a profit and be the leaders in our industry?"

A valuable asset as Head of Distribution, Barb was clearly nervous about the first meeting with the new CEO and she hoped she had passed the quiz. The other leaders offered no further explanation or support.

Dan asked his question a second time, waiting semi-patiently for a response.

Again, silence.

"Do we have a list of published values?" asked the concerned CEO.

Tom Murphy, Director of Human Resources, offered a quick explanation: "Well, you see, Mr. Branston…"

"Please call me Dan. I'm not old enough to be Mr. Branston," interjected Dan quickly, adding specific emphasis on the word "Mr."

Tom, who was noted for his uncanny ability to CYB— "Cover Your Backend"—was visibly shaken.

"Yes, well, Mr. Dan. Are you sure it's alright to call you Dan?" asked the squirming Tom Murphy.

Dan nodded.

"Okay then," Tom continued, "we have values for the organization written in our personnel handbook. But the last CEO told us to stifle the values because they really didn't matter. He told us we were to make money, period."

The rest of the group nodded eagerly in agreement.

"Stifle the values because they really didn't matter," Dan repeated aloud. "Ouch," thought Dan.

As he listened to further comments, explanations, and excuses, Dan realized that this turnaround project was definitely larger than he was.

Something was missing from this group. Clear values and a safe environment were obviously absent elements. But there were other missing pieces. He must get his hands around it. He needed to find the magic bullet. Dan thought back to his office and the elk below his window: "Strength and stamina. I'll definitely need both here."

Dan scratched a note on his yellow tablet: "As safety goes up, so does participation."

The new CEO understood that it would take time to build trust and rapport with his new team. Both elements were essential if he was going to make headway with this group. But the comments, and the lack of leadership, were a cause for concern.

Perhaps his next scheduled meeting would offer more insights. Dan adjourned the meeting and scratched on his tablet, "Values: get'em, grow'em, live by'em."

He was off to the New Employee Orientation meeting. After all, he was the new kid on the block.

Meeting the New Employees...

Sitting amongst twelve rookie employees, the new CEO listened intently to the new employee orientation meeting. To the group, he wasn't the latest CEO; he was just another new hire learning the ropes at BoMar Industries, Ltd.

"The ropes," as it turned out, became a data dump of rules, policies and government forms. Heavy on directives, do's and don'ts, and information overload; light on direction, vision and values. The session failed to reveal how each person in the audience made a positive contribution to the organization.

Dan heard the words from the Leadership Team echo in his mind, "Stifle the values because they really don't matter. He told us we were to make money, period."

No wonder this was perhaps the most inspiration-less orientation he had ever attended.

The new CEO had hoped that each new hire would receive a solid indoctrination into the rich history and proud tradition of BoMar Industries. He had anticipated that each person would walk out the door with a clear understanding of how to win on the BoMar team.

Instead, he experienced a "Here's the rules, there's your desk; if you're here in two weeks, come get a pay check" approach to New Employee Orientation.

Dan made a note on his yellow pad: "Set people up to win from day one."

The new CEO had envisioned a much different orientation approach. His orientation would help new hires feel a part of the team from day one. It would give them a clear vision of where the organization was headed and the importance of each employee's contribution to the success of the company.

New employees would know what was important and how to win with one another from day one.

The session ended. Dan headed for his office. "Strength and stamina," he thought to himself. "And keep breathing! We'll discover the keys to making this place hum again."

"On a positive note, the meeting did feature tasty donuts and drinkable coffee."

Meeting the Customers...

The new CEO reviewed the notes on his yellow pad: "Unreliable, unpredictable, can't count on you, inconsistent, dodge responsibility, condescending, no one will take ownership, confused, argumentative, a 'who cares' attitude, the run around, hard to do business with you, B.Y.W."

Not exactly the comments from your key clients you'd want to collect describing the company. True to his go-getter reputation, Dan spent three days in six cities with the top eight accounts of BoMar Industries. Each visit yielded the same result: "We're not happy. You'd better improve, and improve **FAST!**"

Dan wasn't shocked by his meetings with the key clients. He had expected a variety of complaints and challenges, but he never imagined he'd be raising the red flag on every account.

Dan reflected on one of the meetings earlier in the week. "May I ask you a rather point blank question?" directing his question to the CEO of BoMar's largest client, Linda Johns.

"Sure, fire away. I think we've been pretty candid up to this point," offered Linda.

"After using such a vast array of negative adjectives to describe doing business with our company, " began Dan, "why do you continue to do business with BoMar Industries?"

"Great question," chuckled the client. "Let me assure you it's not because we haven't looked for other resources. In fact, your company still produces the best product for our application, but your competition is hot on your heels. My guess is that within the next 60-90 days, your competition will be able to offer the same product at the same price. I can also guarantee they'll be much easier to do business with."

Dan heard the Linda's message loud and clear. The conversation was anything but hostile or confrontational, simply one CEO speaking to another.

Dan ventured another question, "If you were in my shoes, what would you do to turn things around and earn your business forever?"

Linda leaned back in her chair and considered the question. "If I were in your shoes, what would I do to turn things around and earn my business forever?" She thought carefully about both the question and the answer.

The client leaned forward in her chair and peered directly at Dan. Linda Johns was renowned for her straightforward approach. You never had to guess where you stood with her—she was honest, open, and direct. Under her guidance, vision and persistence, Linda had directed her team and company to number one in the industry. Her company was a best practice model others wanted to emulate.

"That's a great question, Dan. Here's my suggestion," Linda began. "Get everyone on your team committed to doing what they say they'll do in the manner in which they promised it would be handled."

"If we can't count on you folks to come through on commitments and promises, it makes life around here pretty ugly. Our job is to help everyone understand and operate from the term B.Y.W.," explained Linda, spelling out the letters B.Y.W. individually with great emphasis.

"B.Y.W.?" asked Dan as he entered the term on his yellow pad. "Okay, I'm hooked. What does B.Y.W. stand for?"

Linda explained, "B.Y.W. stands for 'Be Your Word.' If your people make a promise to my people—or any other client for that matter—they should remember B.Y.W. This one concept will save both of us hours of headaches and grief. Furthermore, it would keep you from losing customers and bring your company back to a competitive level."

Dan underlined the three letters on his yellow pad.

He reflected on the phrase B.Y.W.—a key to keeping customers happy while reducing headaches and hassles.

Dan thanked his fellow CEO and promised they'd be in touch again, soon.
The flight home was long, not so much in time and distance but rather in contemplation and mental drain.

It had been a stressful first week, he thought to himself. First, the meeting with the Leadership Team or "Lacking Leadership Team"—then the lackluster New Employee Orientation meeting. "No wonder people are walking around aimlessly," Dan mused.

Next came three days on the road, meeting with clients who were less than thrilled about doing business with his company.

"Ugly," thought Dan. "We've got our work cut out for us. There's so much to accomplish. But where do we begin?"

Glancing to his left, he noticed the open page of the magazine being read by the gray haired man beside him. Catching Dan's attention was the full color picture of a bull elk, standing on a ridge, apparently emitting a call.

He took a deep breath and smiled. He had received the message: Strength and Stamina.

Though it had been a long first week, Dan decided to enjoy the rest of his flight home.

Chapter Two
The Broken Boy

The weekend could not have come soon enough. Dan needed to step back from "information overload" and process all he had experienced.

Today was Saturday, but not just any Saturday. It was Volunteer Saturday. Dan looked forward to his one day per month when he took advantage of the opportunity to serve. In fact, volunteering had made such a positive impact on his personal life that he had created a volunteer program at his last company. Everyone was encouraged to take one day per month and volunteer with the organization of his or her choice. And employees received full pay for the day.

Dan knew that his folks would gain far more than they gave through the volunteer experience. Plus there were additional benefits for the company as well: employees returned to their jobs with a recharged spirit, a renewed sense of commitment and enthusiasm for their jobs. It also made a significant impact in the community.

Dan realized that creating the volunteer program was one of the best investments he had made in the turnaround effort at his last company. Perhaps he could instill the same spirit of volunteerism at BoMar Industries, Ltd.

For the last four years, Dan had spent at least one Saturday a month, usually more, working with kids and adults at the Spinal Cord Injury Rehabilitation Center, an organization for people who had suffered a traumatic spinal cord injury. It was a place of extreme emotional highs and lows, from people coming to grips with the extent of their injury to patients taking their first steps after years of rehabilitation, hard work and tears. Above all else, it was a place of hope. Dan looked forward to becoming one piece of hope today.

Dan anticipated working with his good buddy, Byron Mills. Over the last three years, Dan had developed an unusual bond with the passionate, quick-witted and often irreverent 23-year-old Byron. He was a bright, sharp boy filled with promise. Three years ago his world was turned upside down when a freak skate boarding accident left him paralyzed from the waist down.

Dan was working at the center the day Byron arrived. He recalled their first meeting vividly. Byron was much like other first timers—patients going through the gambit of emotions from denial, "why me," and bargaining with God; to fear; to searching for a ray of promise and hope. Hope shined brightly in Byron's eyes.

But Dan remembered looking at the mature, strong boy sitting tall in the wheel chair knowing that Byron was in for the challenge of his life. Dan closed the file on the young man who was both a star athlete and standout student. Approaching the new member of the rehab center he began, "Hi, Byron, I'm Dan Branston. I'm a volunteer here at the center. It'll be my pleasure to assist any way I can in your rehabilitation. Tell me about your accident."

Byron looked trustingly into the eyes of Dan, the Volunteer. His words were spoken with the authority of a person far more mature in years. "It was a freak accident. You couldn't replicate it again in a thousand tries. It was just one of those things."

Byron continued with clarity and conviction, "Sometimes God needs to get you on your back before you start looking up." His eyes glanced heavenward.

Byron paused as if reflecting on the meaning of the accident and his participation at the rehab center today with Dan. He further explained, "I'm not going to pretend I can do it all by myself. Nice to meet you, sir. I guess I'll be counting on lots of people like you while I'm here at the center."

Dan stared intently at Byron for a moment. Gone was the blame, excuses, the "if only I'd of's" which so many other patients brought to the center. "Could this young man be only 20?" thought Dan.

From deep in thought, he snapped to and returned to the present moment. "It has been a long couple of years for my friend," reflected Dan. The goal of helping Byron walk again made his Saturday visits all the more meaningful.

Today was a special day at the rehab center for many of the patients. They were going to "swing through the air with the greatest of ease." Today they would become Flying Trapeze Artists. Under the strict supervision of a rather innovative and forward thinking circus performer, patients from the rehab center would be taken to the Circus Big Top and given the chance to "perform."

Initially, Dan had expressed extreme concern for what he called the "stunt," but the director of the rehab center had reassured Dan and others that the utmost precautions had been considered. Only those physically able, with reliable upper body strength and coordination, would be allowed to participate. Dan was now rather intrigued by the concept and looked forward to participating and learning.

The Trapeze Buddy Success Strategy

The activity was the brainchild of Flying Trapeze artist Alex Aims, who considered the trapeze a great place for patients to build confidence and trust. It would be the perfect place to confront their fears and, more importantly, move through those fears. Being high above the circus floor offered the participants new perspectives and fresh possibilities—and it just might be a load of fun.

Alex and his team had devised a special safety harness for moving patients to and from the trapeze platform, a tiny board some fifty feet above the ground. Dan concluded that merely reaching the platform should be considered a major victory. After all, fifty feet was the equivalent of five stories above the ground! And the platform was anything but BIG.

Each junior trapeze artist would wear a safety harness the entire time he was in the air. For added safety, two people on the ground would anchor each "flyer," like mountain climbers belaying their partners.

The set-up sounded impressive for both the participant and the spectators, who would be comprised of the patient's family and friends.

"So where are your tights, Mr. Trapeze man?" Byron taunted Dan in his customary lighthearted manner. "You ready to fly today?" Byron continued to torment his friend.

"Oh darn, I left my tights at the cleaners," retorted Dan. "I guess you'll have to do the flying for both of us."

Both men laughed with a good natured spirit shared only between close friends.

Byron was ready to face this new adventure as he had everything else at the center. "Bring it on" became his war cry. Mr. Cool, Calm and Collected. Right!

Alex, the Flying Trapeze Artist, had explained the entire process to the "novice Trapeze Artist." In theory, each participant understood what they would encounter at the Big Top.

The director of the rehab center reviewed the key points with the group before loading the bus—more for her nerves than those of the participants. "Each person will have the opportunity to swing from the trapeze. You will be wearing a safety harness any time your feet are off the ground. It's your choice to participate or return to the ground. Your safety is our utmost concern."

"It's our hope that this will be a memorable and meaningful experience for each person. Remember to have some fun and smile; we'll be video taping the entire performance," she admonished.

"Does my hair look okay for the camera?" Byron asked Dan playfully. "Make sure they get a picture of my good side."

Both men chuckled.

"Are you ready?" asked Dan.

"I think I'm ready," explained the young, soon-to-be trapeze artist, "but then again, I'm not really sure what I'm supposed to be ready for. I guess I'll take it one swing at a time," he concluded. "A little trapeze humor—one swing at a time."

The bus ride to the Big Top was buzzing with nervous anticipation.

"You can't fly a kite unless you go against the wind and have a weight to keep it from turning somersaults. The same with man. No man will succeed unless he is ready to face and overcome difficulties and is prepared to assume responsibilities."

– *William J. H. Boetcker*

Chapter Three
Dropped Again!

"Swing from the air with the greatest of ease. Yeah, right!" muttered Byron to himself.

Sitting below the trapeze safety net, Byron took in the entire process. He noticed the personal safety harness system and located the hoist to lift his partially functioning frame to the performance platform. He spied several more assistants on the platform. There was the trapeze swing gizmo (lots of unfamiliar items looked like gizmos to Byron); a second trapeze swing gizmo for the second trapeze artist—this person would undoubtedly be the "catcher." Byron eyed two belayers who stood firmly planted on the earth ready to "catch" Byron should he fail to make the connection with his appointed trapeze partner; and, of course, there was the safety net.

"It's your turn. Are you ready?" asked an unfamiliar voice. Byron snapped out of his daze and returned to planet Earth.

"Ready?" Byron asked rather than stated. "Yeah. Sure. I guess I'm ready," he said uncertainly. "Let's do it. I think. Or, do I really want to do this?" Byron could feel his heart beginning to race—and his mind chattering in non-stop dialogue like an annoying pest. The small voice ranted in one giant, run-on sentence. "After all, it's a looong way up to the platform and you've never done this before and besides your legs don't work and I'm sure you need two strong legs to make this thing work and then there is the matter of…"

"Shut up!" Byron commanded the little voice in his head, which seemed to be working overtime.

Both circus assistants waited for Byron to answer his own question. They were perfectly content to await Byron's choice to participate. They also understood his degree of resignation, resistance, hesitation— downright fear! It was part of the territory, a regular feature of the process.

Byron held up both thumbs. "Okay, let's do it. Here goes nothing!" He was attempting, without much success, to align the butterflies in his stomach to fly in formation.

The circus assistants carefully attached the specially designed safety harness around Byron. They checked it, then double checked it. Byron was invited to review the work, and a representative of the rehab center verified that everything was in operational order. No one was going to take any unnecessary risks.

Two cables were attached to Byron's safety harness at the chest. The circus assistants explained, in exacting detail, the next steps. Byron nodded his understanding, his butterflies batting their wings at a record pace. More like hummingbirds than butterflies!

"He's yours," shouted the circus assistant as Byron felt the cables tug at his harness. He was beginning to levitate out of his chair, heading skyward.

Up to this point, Byron understood the trapeze concept in theory. He had accepted the concept, but retained the standard fears and reservations. Now, with his legs dangling high above the floor, theory was being transformed into experience. He looked at his wheelchair—ten feet away, then 15, now 25, suddenly 40 feet below him.

"Byron, you're almost here," a reassuring voice resonated from above. Byron was in a daze, staring down at the tiny little "how could anyone sit in that miniature wheelchair?" some 50 feet below.

"Got ya!" the two platform assistants sang in unison. Music to Byron's ears. The assistants sat Byron on the edge of the platform. "Take a minute to look around and soak in the site from 50 feet above the circus floor," instructed one of the assistants. "Notice all the people looking at you from below."

Byron steadied himself with the support of the assistants and noted the world buzzing below him. Worker ants were apparently busy getting things ready for the show. He noticed his parents in the stands and offered a faint wave. Then he spotted the belayers at their station, the spotlight operator, the other trapeze artist across the way. Several of his buddies from the rehab center down below attracted his attention, and he saw Dan getting hooked up in his safety harness preparing for his turn on the flying trapeze—after Byron's performance.

Byron nodded when he had completed the preflight safety check. His heart was beating faster than before.

"The first thing we want to do is help you become comfortable with the process," explained the platform assistant. "This is your trapeze bar. It'll become your new best friend," he added as he handed Byron the bar.

The platform coach continued with the lesson. "The first step will be for you to experience how it feels to swing on the trapeze. When you give us the "Go" sign, we'll push you off the platform. Your job is to swing out to the center on your trapeze bar and then let it carry you back to the platform. We'll grab you and place your bottom back on the platform. Pretty simple, right?"

Byron confirmed, "You're going to push me off this perfectly good platform from some 50 feet above the ground. I'm supposed to hang on and swing out there. Then you're going to catch me and put my bottom back down on this perfectly solid platform? Man, they call me the 'Ice Man' back at the center," confessed Byron. "I'm usually cool, calm and collected. But I've got to admit that I feel anything but Ice Man-ish right now. Puddle Man perhaps, but definitely not Ice Man."

Both coaches laughed. They remembered the feeling.

"I think I've got it. I hope I've got it," answered the non-Ice Man.

The platform coach confirmed, "Sounds like you understand. Pretty simple."

Byron did another quick assessment: harness was still attached, the belayers were awake and ready. The trapeze seemed to be hooked to something, his heart was still beating, and the butterflies were in full rage. He nodded his ready sign.

Over the loudspeaker he heard an announcer declare, "And now, ladies and gentlemen, turn your eyes to the platform high above the circus floor and watch as Byron Wells defies gravity on his flying trapeze." A sudden burst of applause erupted from the enthusiastic audience. Byron felt the need to offer his adoring fans a slight wave—a very slight wave!

When Byron shouted, "GO!" the assistants pushed him from his perch. He felt the swift glide of the trapeze as it headed for the center of the ring. It paused momentarily, and then he sensed that he was gliding backwards, returning to the platform. Four hands quickly guided him to his seat. "Caught. Just like they promised," Byron muttered under his breath.

Then an elated Byron shouted, "WOW! I did it!" Applause exploded from the audience. Now willing to play along and ham it up a bit, Byron waved to his adoring fans.

"Good job," offered one of the assistants with absolute encouragement. "Pretty simple, wasn't it?"

"Now we want to add the next element," suggested the second platform coach. "This time we're going to time our push with the other trapeze artist across the way."

Byron looked up and noticed a huge guy standing on the opposite platform with a trapeze in hand.

"The goal is to meet in the center and lightly touch," explained the platform coach. "Don't let go, and don't do any fancy spins or tricks; just swing out to the center and lightly touch. Got it?"

Byron's mind was racing. The phrase "touch lightly" was cause for alarm. On his last swing he had reached speeds exceeding 250 miles per hour—okay, perhaps not 250, but it felt that fast! He also viewed the other artist as about 12 times his size and weight, and he saw no brakes to control the speed on his trapeze bar.

"Touch lightly?" Byron asked.

"Yes. The trapeze is designed to reach a certain point," patiently explained the platform coach. "If you've timed it right and meet in the center, you should touch lightly."

"And if we don't meet in the center, do we collide, crash and burn?" asked Byron, attempting to add some levity to the challenge before him.

The instructor chuckled. "If you don't meet in the center, it means we didn't push you hard enough off this platform. It also suggests that we try it again until we get it right. Lightly touch, that's our goal. Got it? You give us the 'Go' sign."

Recalculating the situation, and rechecking all his gear and support systems, Byron gave the "thumbs up."

Like magic, the announcer again drew everyone's attention to Byron. Sitting high above the circus floor, he offered his fans a nod of acknowledgement.

The platform assistants counted one, two, three while making hand signals to the other trapeze artist. Byron felt the push from behind and headed straight for the 375 pound, muscle bound trapeze equivalent of Godzilla. The two lightly touched although Byron had closed his eyes in case it would help to avoid a head-on collision. Swinging back to the platform, he was recaptured by his two partners.

"Great timing, you did it!" celebrated one of the assistants.

"High five, it was perfect," offered the second coach.

A round of high fives circled the platform, and applause exploded from the audience below. Byron was getting into the spirit; these folks were acting as if they were really impressed. Byron was definitely impressed. He had "lightly" touched the monster man.

"What's next?" asked a rapidly breathing Byron.

"Now the fun begins," suggested one platform coach as the other coach nodded in agreement. "You get to swing out there, let go and get caught by your trapeze partner from across the way. Pretty simple, right?"

Byron's eyes dilated to the size of basketball hoops. "I'm supposed to be pushed off this perfectly solid platform, swing out to the middle on what appears to be a perfectly fine trapeze, and let go so some guy hanging upside down in tights can catch me? Yeah, right!"

"You've got it down perfectly. If the timing is right, the two of you will catch one another. Remember, when you let go of the bar, your job is to find your partner's hands. He'll also be looking for yours. You catch each other, and he'll hold most of the weight," the coach instructed.

Suddenly, Byron was glad to be playing catch with Godzilla, the 350 pound, muscle bound Trapeze artist. "Is he any good at catching?" quizzed Byron. "He's not blind in one eye or suffering from a disability like mine, is he?"

"He's the best in the business. You'll be in good hands. Almost sounds like a commercial." The two coaches chuckled at their play on words.

"Are you ready?" Byron suddenly wanted to recheck the entire operation, especially the two belayers below. They appeared to be awake and alert.

"*If* the timing is right, we're *supposed to* catch each other," Byron commented under his breath, adding special emphasis to the words "if" and "supposed to."

His review was complete. "Ready!" Byron yelled. "GO!"

On cue, the announcer once more directed the audience's attention to the platform high above the circus floor. "And now, ladies and gentlemen, Byron Wells will attempt a death defying release and catch with his trapeze partner, Alex."

The applause increased from below.

Byron thought, "The announcer guy could lose the 'death defying' stuff." He was now totally focused on the task at hand: swing, release, catch; swing, release, catch.

Feeling the push at his back, he was suddenly flying through the air with a death grip on the bar, knuckles white, his heart roaring. Byron approached the center and released the bar, searching for a friendly set of big hands. He spotted them and reached, but they weren't close enough. He was too far away; he couldn't make the grab. He was rocketing toward the net!

"Many people want to change their results but they are unwilling to change themselves, so they therefore remain bound."
– *James Allen*

Chapter Four
Being Caught Is A Whole Lot More Fun

Screams of utter terror penetrated every corner of the Big Top and as far away as the next state. Byron's lungs could register his abject terror!

In what appeared to be slow motion, Byron extended his upper body with everything he had. His hands reached out and brushed the extended fingertips of his partner, but they had missed each other. Byron had been dropped and was plummeting toward the floor. As he began to anticipate a crushing encounter with the concrete below, his harness jerked him back to reality. He was alive. He wasn't going to die. Not yet, anyway.

The safety harness and cargo were hoisted slowly back to the platform where Byron's coaches awaited his return.

"Awesome, perfect, right on target," cheered one of the coaches. "And nice scream, too! We love people who really put passion into everything they do!" added the other coach.

Byron cleared his head and observed, "It didn't look too perfect to me. We barely even touched, let alone caught each other."

The coaches nodded. "You're right, it's not perfect yet. But you see, we never identify a miss as a failure. We see it as a 'Great Moment.' We tried something, we got some feedback about whether we're on target, and now we can make the needed adjustments. It's a great moment when you get all the information and feedback in one little swing."

Byron considered the Great Moment definition. He understood the intent, yet protested, "But we didn't catch one another. What did I do wrong?"

"You tell us. What PLUS 10% adjustments would you make so you're caught more and dropped less?"

"PLUS 10%?" pondered Byron. "What little adjustments could I make to move performance to the next level? I suppose I could wait a split second or two before I released the bar." His enthusiasm increased; the light bulb had turned on. "If I get a bit higher, then release, it'll give us both time to spot each other as I fall."

"Right on target!" a coach responded. "Any other PLUS 10% adjustments?"

Byron considered the question before answering again. "I suppose we could confirm our timing by communicating exactly when I was going to leave this comfortable little platform."

"Good, go on. Are there more adjustments you could make in order to increase the odds of being caught more and dropped less?"

"I think that's about it, other than practice together and give it another shot," Byron continued. He scooted himself closer toward the edge of the platform. "In fact, let's give it another shot. This time we're going to get it."

The coaches confirmed his readiness. It was thumbs up from across the safety net; Godzilla was ready. Byron looked at his harness and the belayers. Everything was in working order. He gave the thumbs up sign.

Perhaps "thumbs up" was the clue for the announcer. One more time a booming voice emulated from the loudspeakers. Byron was beginning to realize that this was an important part of the act. He waited for the announcement, then offered a wave to the crowd below.

"One, two, three," and off he went. His eyes were unusually wide open during this swing. He was clear on his intention: swing out there, get some height, release and make the catch. "Make the catch, make the catch" became his silent mantra.

Byron zipped across on his trapeze, heading for center stage. Resisting the urge to release, he hung in there for what seemed like at least a good half hour to forty-five minutes. Then he released, this time substantially higher than last time. His body seemed to float as it paused at the top of his release. He spotted the outstretched hands of Godzilla, extended his arms in an effort to be caught, and began to fall. Life seemed to be moving in slow motion. He wanted hands to connect, yet everything was moving much too slowly. The hands of Godzilla came into position, fully extended, but Byron was too far above his partner to make the catch. The hands he wanted to catch moved away. He reached but to no avail—once again a fingertip touch. He had missed again! He'd been dropped and was heading for the safety net. Finally he felt the familiar tug of the safety harness. He had survived again.

"Another Great Moment?" Byron asked with some degree of failure in his voice.

"I don't know, was it?" asked a coach. "Looked pretty impressive from here. It's only a Great Moment if you learn something from the experience. If you don't learn anything, it's a heavy duty mistake."

Byron knew the next step would be up to him. What PLUS 10% adjustments would he make in order to produce the desired result?

"Let's start with this question," began a coach. "What did you do RIGHT last time? What worked?"

Considering the question, Byron offered, "My timing was close but just a hair off this time."

"Good, we'll talk about that issue in a minute. What else worked?"

"I think I got pretty good height during the swing. At least I seemed to hang around for a solid forty-five minutes to three hours," reflected Byron. "I think my speed was pretty good, and I must say, I was willing to swing out there."

"All good points. So what will you do differently this time in order to produce a different result?" quizzed the coach. "Talk to me about your height and the timing issue."

The Trapeze Buddy Success Strategy

Byron pondered the question. He knew that his insight would be key to making the catch.

The rookie trapeze artist began, "I went higher this time, but in an effort to look for my partner's hands longer, I threw off his timing. He swung out there based on where I had been last time. I told you two about my new plan but failed to alert one of the most important people in making this show work. A minor oversight," Byron offered with mock amusement.

The two coaches high-fived each other in agreement. "By jove, I think he's got it," one coach offered in a rather weak English accent. "Let's put it all together and make it work this time."

The coach flashed several hand signals across the performance arena, and Alex returned the "Okay" sign from his perch.

"Alex understands the plan and will expect you to be where you were last time. Same height, same speed. He'll swoop in and catch you," instructed the coach. "One more little detail might assist you: look for his wrists. Try to grab him around the wrists, not just the hands. You'll have more catching power. Focus on the wrists."

With this last nugget of coaching, the artists looked toward each other. The "Go" signal was given, the announcer chimed in across the loudspeaker, and Byron waved, but this time focusing less on the wave and more on the task at hand.

"Swing, Release, Catch," the silent mantra began. The swing proceeded much like the last attempt, with Byron resisting the release until the trapeze had reached its highest point on the arch. Upon his release, he began the immediate scan for two large, taped wrists. Plummeting toward the safety net, his eyes zeroed in on the target, and he reached for the rapidly approaching paws.

"Come on, come on," Byron uttered in a mild panic, "get over here." Before he could finish the statement, his arms and torso jerked as Alex landed his prey — two sets of gigantic hands grasping two sets of significantly smaller wrists. The grip was a magical sight to Byron's eyes. Mission accomplished! He was an official junior trapeze artist. He'd been caught!

The crowd came unglued as Byron was lowered to the safety net. A smile spreading from ear to ear, he acknowledged the applause of the supportive crowd. He waved to his platform coaches and Alex, the Godzilla of the Trapeze. He also took a quick moment to acknowledge himself. He had been willing to swing out there and be caught, fulfilling the task in spite of his fear and anxiety.

He was a Flying Trapeze Artist!

The event turned out to be magical for performers, audience members and volunteers alike. What had once been a wild idea by a circus performer had become a breakthrough opportunity for all involved.

If the bus ride to the circus had been buzzing with nervous anticipation, the ride home was levitating with wild enthusiasm. Participants shared countless stories of fear, determination, and the rush of doing something they thought was impossible just hours earlier. They also marveled at the expertise of the Flying Trapeze Troupe, from dealing with the unique challenges of each participant to the thrilling show they offered at the conclusion of the day.

"Did you see the size of your eyes?" asked Dan. "They were the size of frying pans!"

"See my eyes? Heck no! All I could hear was my heart racing 147,000 miles an hour," responded a fired-up Byron. "I'm surprised you couldn't hear my heart pounding from where you were sitting! And you should have seen your eyes and the death grip you had on the bar. I thought you would never let go!"

Dan sat filled with excitement, emotion and disbelief. He had just witnessed what many would consider the impossible. Paraplegic boys, girls, men and women flying high above the circus floor, as well as one nervous CEO.

The expression in the eyes of the participants told the entire story. A story of dream, dare and trust.

Dan was confident that the participants would never be the same after swinging out from the skinny platform, then letting go at just the right moment. The roar from the audience was still ringing in his ears.

Dan and Byron discussed the adventure at length. Byron noted, "I could hardly believe how tightly everyone needed to work together to make our show happen. If you consider all the hands involved—from the spotters to the music, the spotlights, the announcer, and our trapeze coaches—it was a huge production. Gosh, if you think about it, even the people who put up the ladders and attached the trapeze had a big hand in the process. And you'd want to include the folks who prepared the grandstands so my parents could sit and share the experience," Byron continued.

"There's an interesting statement," Dan interrupted. "What started you thinking along those lines?"

"Well," began Byron, "I was planning to write a thank you note to everyone who made today possible, but the more I thought about it, the longer the list kept growing. It took the imagination, commitment, dedication and talent of many people to take some cables, the net, a selection of music and a safety harness and turn it all into magic. We couldn't have done it without everyone being a Trapeze Buddy to everyone in the show."

"Sure, I was counting on Godzilla to catch me as I let go of the bar," recalled Byron, "but I was also depending on a bunch of other people to come through today. Without their part there would have been no show. I had scores of Trapeze Buddies out there. Trapeze Buddies," mused Byron. "People I count on every day. Now that I think about it, I rely on people back at the rehab center as well. I guess you could call them my Trapeze Buddies, too."

Dan stared in amazement at his young friend. "Far beyond his years," he thought to himself. He reflected on Byron's example and insight.

Then it suddenly hit him. Byron's words continued to ring in his ears.

"Perhaps this is the metaphor I need for BoMar Industries," thought the CEO. "Trapeze Buddies. Being caught more by the people you count on every day."

Turning to his paraplegic friend, a reflective CEO announced, "You know everyone's a teacher, and I was just offered another life lesson from you."

The day ended with high fives, big grins and enthusiastic hugs. Multiple seeds of possibility had been planted.

"By perseverance the snail reached the ark."
— *Charles H. Spurgeon*

Chapter Five
Mind Mapping

The following day Dan returned to the rehab center to meet with Byron. He had spent the evening jotting note after note on his yellow pad and was eager to run his new learning past his Trapeze Buddy.

The rehab center was still buzzing after last night's performance and a new bounce seemed to register in everyone's spirit. Dan noticed Byron and two of his fellow "flyers" chatting in the corner. Judging by the hand and arm gestures, he was certain the conversation revolved around swinging out on the trapeze, letting go and being caught.

"Morning, guys," Dan greeted the trio. Warm hellos were accompanied by a series of "high fives" for Dan—a customary greeting.

"You three are still buzzing from last night."

Heads nodded in complete agreement.

"I know. I couldn't sleep! I stayed up and wrote some notes about the experience and our conversation after the show," Dan said as he glanced at Byron. "Can I run a couple things by the three of you and get your input and ideas?"

An enthusiastic "Sure" rang out from the trio, and the boys leaned forward in their wheelchairs, listening for Dan's next words.

Dan picked up his notes and turned to Byron. "I was thinking about your insight into the number of people it took to pull off last night's show. If you were to write a thank you note to each person, the list would be pretty extensive. You used a phrase which impressed upon me the importance of people working together to 'put on a great show.'"

"I used the phrase 'Trapeze Buddies,'" Byron explained to his two partners, Tony and Scott. "A Trapeze Buddy is anyone we counted on last night to come through so we could put on a great show. The list was pretty long—lighting people, music, the set-up crew, costumers, the actual flying artists, the safety harness folks, and the announcer guy who kept proclaiming the death defying stunt—to name just a few."

Dan picked up the ball from there. "Exactly. We all counted on lots of folks to put on a good show. I was thinking you guys have 'Trapeze Buddies' here at the rehab center, too—people you count on every day."

All three nodded in agreement, waiting for Dan to proceed. "I started to make a list on paper—I call it Mind Mapping. I wanted to capture in visual form all the people you rely on for rehab—your Trapeze Buddies."

Dan paused a moment for the idea to settle in. Then he asked, "Could you help me create a list and fill in the circles using all your Trapeze Buddies here at the center?"

Heads nodded as the trio approved the request.

"To begin with," began Scott, "there are the PTs."

"Physical Therapists," Dan muttered aloud, entering a note on his yellow pad.

"As a semi-outsider, you might identify them as Physical Therapists but around here we lovingly refer to them as the physical torturers," Scott smiled wryly.

The other boys nodded in enthusiastic agreement. "You're right about that!" endorsed Tony. "Pain and torture is their middle name."

The insiders understood that the job of the PT was to push the patients beyond their comfort zones—to the point of pain, fatigue and exhaustion. Thus they earned their respected nickname.

"Was I set up for that one or what?" asked Dan. "I've changed the heading to just plain PT. Physical torturers. That's cute, real cute."

"Good start. Who else serves as a Trapeze Buddy?" encouraged Dan.

Tony commented, "How about the cafeteria? Are there Trapeze Buddies there?"

"Sure," chimed in Byron. "Remember, our definition is anyone whom we count on or who relies on us. And since it's about 20 minutes until lunch, I think I'm counting on the cafeteria folks big time."

"Great, I'll include the cafeteria," noted Dan. "By the way, any pet names for the cafeteria folks? No, wait, I'm sure you have some frightening names with this wild group, so forget the question."

"He knows us all too well," chuckled Scott.

"Okay, I have two Trapeze Buddies so far. Who else?"

"The doctors, the nurses and the people who maintain the equipment," Scott added.

Dan wrote quickly.

"Yeah, and there's the lifeguard at the pool," shot in Tony. "And don't forget the van drivers who pick us up from our homes. You'll also want to add our parents to the list." Tony was proud of his contribution.

"Good additions," Dan noted as he wrote lifeguards, van drivers, parents.

Byron added his perspective. "How about the volunteers like you, Dan, and the janitor team? With these two slobs here, it's more than a full time job," Byron quipped.

Scott and Tony responded with a volley of disdain and a few loving thumps to Byron's head.

"We have a few more Trapeze Buddies," Byron blurted in an attempt to stifle the barrage of rebellion. "There are the insurance people who pay the bills, the administrative people who handle the paper work, and even the other patients. We count on each other mutually for encouragement and friendship."

Byron smiled and paused in a moment of devilish reflection. "Encouragement and friendship, except from these goons. They're pretty lifeless." Byron received more playful blows to the head from Scott and Tony and this time Dan added a few shots of his own to the squirrelly character.

"Excellent. We've got a good list started here."

Dan reviewed the list of Trapeze Buddies compiled so far: "PTs, cafeteria people, doctors, nurses, maintenance people, lifeguard, van drivers, parents, volunteers, janitorial team, insurance people, administrative folks, and other patients. Pretty good for a two minute focus. Well, thanks fellas. You three are obviously ready for lunch."

Glancing at his notes, Dan reflected, "I imagine if we took additional time, we'd uncover even more Trapeze Buddies and could add them to our list." The boys watched with amusement as Dan played out his mental gymnastics. "Every company could do this exercise and create its own list of Trapeze Buddies. In fact, every department could make a list of its Trapeze Buddies."

Byron interrupted Dan's focus. "And remember the costume person as one of your Trapeze Buddies."

Dan looked puzzled.

Byron waited for the comment to sink in before offering the punch line. "You looked darn cute in those lavender tights last night. Your costume creating Trapeze Buddy did a marrrrrrrvelous job."

Dan reached to thump Byron's head, but all three boys were already racing down the hall, headed for the cafeteria. They had become rather proficient in their wheelchairs.

"Cute. Real cute," reflected an amused Dan.

"Security is mostly a superstition. It does not exist in nature, nor do the children of men as a whole experience it. Avoiding danger is no safer in the long run than outright exposure. Life is either a daring adventure, or nothing."
– *Helen Keller*

Chapter Six
C.A.T.C.H Technology

Trapeze Buddies. It has an interesting ring to it, thought the new CEO.

As Dan picked up the phone, he reflected on the idea; it just made sense; it was a piece of the puzzle missing at BoMar Industries. Dan wondered how far he could carry this metaphor and its potential impact on his organization.

A voice on the other end of the phone announced, "Thanks for calling Flying Aces. This is Alex. How might I be of assistance?"

Dan introduced himself as the guy who was scared to death as he swung from the trapeze. He was with Byron and other folks from the Spinal Cord Injury Rehab Center.

Alex chuckled and responded in a good natured tone, "Oh, I remember you. It's not often I see eyeballs the size of car tires. And was that you yelling for your mom to rescue you?"

Both men roared with laughter.

"That was me alright," admitted Dan. "Did I whimper too much in front of the children?"
"That's why we have bull horns. The children need to hear the instruction over the cries of the adults."

"Good thinking and a much needed tool. Let me tell you why I called," began Dan. "First off, I was really impressed with what you did with those kids. You should have heard the bus ride back to the center. The kids were beaming. It opened whole new possibilities for them. And your contribution was significant."

"Thank you," Alex replied. "It's simply our way of giving back. As you know from your work with both kids and adults, we always seem to receive a lot more than we give. It's nice to hear that we opened some opportunities."

"Amen!" chimed in Dan. "I look forward to my visits more than I can tell you. They never seem to be convenient, but I walk away with my battery charged, feeling like I made a small difference."

"Speaking of making a difference," continued the CEO, "I need your help on another matter."

"Wait a minute," quipped Alex, "I can help paraplegic kids swing with the greatest of ease, but I'm not sure I can add you to our show."

"It's nothing that impossible," chuckled Dan. "But it is pretty challenging. I want to learn how to be a Trapeze Artist, or what I'm now calling a Trapeze Buddy. I want to discover what it takes to put on a perfect show, night after night, then apply those same principles to my business organization."

The phone fell silent.

"So you want to be a 'Trapeze Buddy' at your company?" Alex asked more as a statement than a question.

"Exactly. As Trapeze artists, your group must operate in a certain way to produce such spectacular results. The same is true in business. If we fail to come through and drop someone, it can get pretty ugly. We can glean many examples from you."

"I never looked at it quite that way," admitted Alex, "but it sounds intriguing."

"Come by Friday afternoon at 2 p.m." continued Alex, "and you can be a part of our rehearsal and get a behind-the-scenes look at how we operate.

Afterwards we can grab a 7 UP and explore your concept further."

"I'll see you Friday!" Dan replied enthusiastically.

"Oh, and one last thing," suggested Alex, "bring your workout clothes. We just might add you to the show. It could be a new comedy skit."

Both men chuckled as they said their goodbyes.

Dan immediately picked up the phone and made one last call to the Spinal Cord Injury Rehab Center. He wanted his Trapeze Buddy, Byron, with him at the rehearsal.

At the Big Top...

Dan and Byron arrived at "Big Top Tent" in time for the rehearsal. Alex was on hand to offer his enthusiastic greeting.

"Did you bring your tights?" Alex ribbed Dan.

"Darn, I left them on my desk at the office. I guess you'll have to do the show without me."

Both men laughed. They had quickly developed a comfortable ease and mutual respect for one another.

"We're about ready to begin our practice," said Alex. "Here's how I suggest you look at the rehearsal: focus more on how we operate together and less on the stunts."

"Less on the stunts?" questioned Dan. "I'm not sure I understand what you mean."

"The stunts are the by-product of the work. If we operate together we'll have a great show. If pieces are missing, it'll appear in the stunts," explained Alex. "Afterwards, let's review your observations."

"We use a concept called 'CATCH.' Everyone on the team understands its importance and is committed to making 'CATCH' work. See if you can identify the elements associated with our acronym," Alex began.

"I can spot one important element right off the bat," chimed in a confident Byron.

Both men waited patiently as the young man drew out his dramatic pause for added effect.

"If you don't 'C.A.T.C.H.,' it can get really 'U.G.L.Y.,'" Byron explained with a grin.

The two adults groaned but recognized the truth of his statement.

"With that pearl of wisdom, I am off to do my part," retorted Alex. "Watch carefully and see what you can discover."

Both Dan and Byron found the rehearsal fascinating. Dan took feverish notes as Byron observed with keen interest and delight, noting, "I never realized so much went on behind the scenes to make the show work."

Byron listened as the music crew practiced a number that would establish the mood of the show. The lighting team added its expertise in order to highlight the artists, and the person in charge of costumes laid out each article in sequence.

Dan watched the team's interaction carefully. They didn't just climb the ladder and begin jumping and spinning. There was a plan, communication, feedback and clarity as to the desired outcome. He added more notes to his yellow pad.

The rehearsal lasted for about two hours—significantly longer than the thirty minute show performed by the troupe three times a day every weekend. It was a workout!

The rehearsal was filled with thrilling stunts, frequent drops and the evolution of a new routine not quite ready for public eyes. It was far from perfect—just a rehearsal.

Alex approached the intrigued observers while toweling off his perspiring brow.

"That was awesome!" exclaimed young Byron. "You guys are really hot!"

"Thank you!" a smiling Alex responded. "I'm feeling REALLY hot after that rehearsal." He continued to mop his forehead, "Let's get a drink and see what you discovered."

The trio moved toward a side area with Dan helping Byron negotiate several obstacles in his wheelchair.

"What do you think 'CATCH' means to our team?" Alex inquired. "Let's begin with the letter, 'C.'"

"I imagine it could stand for a variety of topics. Here's a few items I observed," began Dan. "I'm going to say that the first 'C' stands for at least two items: 'Commitment' and 'Communication.' Without commitment from everyone on the team, you don't stand a chance! It's only a matter of time before someone gets dropped and the show is a bust."

Alex offered an affirming nod.

Dan continued, "I noticed a high degree of communication between team members. In fact, it was some of the most exacting, precise, leave-no-room-for-errors communication I've ever observed."

"You're right on the money," responded Alex. "Those are two important elements to our success—two keys to being good Trapeze Buddies."

"I'll jot those on the white board," offered Alex. He picked up a marker and wrote a large letter 'C.' Next to the letter he listed "**Commitment**" and "**Communication**."

"What do you think 'A' stands for in our little phrase?" questioned Alex.

Byron quickly chimed in, "It's got to stand for 'accuracy.'" You can't put on a good show without a high degree of exactness. In fact, I noticed that the big drops happened because you were only a few inches off on accuracy. 'Close-but-no-cigar,' as we say at the rehab center."

"The other night," continued Byron, "I touched fingers twice but was dropped both times. We were close but lacked the accuracy needed to make a full connection."

"Close, but no cigar," offered Dan.

"So 'A' stands for 'Accuracy'?" questioned Alex.

"Absolutely," responded a confident Byron. "Just try doing a show without it. I think you'd get 'U.G.L.Y.' instead of awesome."

"I get your point," chuckled Alex. "And, I must admit, you're right on target. Let's add it to our list."

Alex added a second letter to the white board, writing a large 'A' with the word "**Accuracy**" next to it.

He then took his marker and wrote a large 'T' on the board. "Okay, students, you're two for two so far. What are we going to put on the board for 'T'?"

Sensing Alex's playful nature, Dan raised his hand in enthusiastic response.

"I know, I know," Dan chirped. "Call on me."

Alex and Byron laughed. "Yes, Dan?" asked Alex.

"Well, from what I saw 'T' has to stand for 'Trust.' Before I would ever climb up there and swing from the platform, I'd want to have a high degree of trust in each of my Trapeze Buddies."

"Excellent. Go on."

"I'm not expecting every person in my business to be perfect on every move, every single show. I guarantee, however, that I'd demand a high degree of trust in their ability and commitment before I'd let go of the trapeze."

"You're right on target," Alex returned. "I'll write '**Trust**' next to our 'T.' It's certainly critical to our success. Trust doesn't mean that I want to party with the performers after the show, but it does mean that if they promise to be there, I can count on it happening. And I know they'll come to the show with a high degree of commitment," Alex added pointing back to the word "commitment."

"What else might 'T' stand for?" asked Alex.

"'T' must also stand for 'Timing,'" Byron submitted.

The two students nodded in agreement.

Byron continued, "Look at your show. If timing is off by a fraction, the results can be…"

"Wait, we know," Dan quickly interjected, and both men simultaneously yelled, "'U.G.L.Y.'!"

All three laughed heartily.

"I think you're beginning to catch on," said Byron. "Back to the show the other night. I threw off the timing because I tried something different and didn't communicate it to Alex, my Trapeze Buddy."

Dan reflected aloud, "The same holds true in my business. If we're off on our timing with other departments or co-workers, we're likely to frustrate the timing of our customers. It can really be…" and all three proclaimed in unison, "U.G.L.Y.!"

Alex added "**Timing**" to the list.

"What else does 'C.A.T.C.H.' stand for? We've covered the first three letters: **Commitment**, **Communication**; **Accuracy**; **Trust** and **Timing**."
Byron offered a guess, "Confidence?"

"That's certainly helpful," replied Alex, "but on the platform we stress another word. It might not be as obvious as the first three letters, so allow me to explain. Each trick or stunt has three phases—a beginning, a middle and an end. If a performer doesn't complete the full cycle—he pulls out, bails or just doesn't make it—the stunt is guaranteed to fail. Furthermore, if everyone on the team doesn't offer complete commitment and communication, we're likely to have a breakdown somewhere down the road." He pointed to the words on the white board.

"Complete!" hollered Byron. "That's the next 'C.' 'Complete.' Write it down," instructed Byron, proud that he was quicker on the draw than his buddy Dan.

"If I don't 'complete' my therapy and workouts, I can't expect to reach my goals," reflected Byron. "I've got to do a 'complete' job every day."

"That's the same for our organization," added Dan. "We can be committed, accurate and have great timing, but if we get only a part of the story or information, we're headed for disaster."

"You guys are on a roll," Alex observed as he added the word "**Complete**" to the white board. "So what shall we do with the 'H' in our word 'CATCH'? You seem to be on top of this word game."

Both students pondered the letter 'H' but seemed to draw a blank.

""Helpful,' 'heroic,' 'happy,' 'hurry'—I want to be caught?" Byron guessed.

"How about 'High Five'? There were plenty of them the other night," Dan said hesitantly.

"Nice try. I could place each of those offerings on the board, but that's not the 'H' word I'm looking for. Our 'H' stands for '**Hang-in-there**'! In our business it's important to understand that not everything will be perfect every time. It's going to take work, practice, minor and sometimes major adjustments to put on a great show. The entire team has to 'hang-in-there' when we've made the catch and 'hang-in-there' as we figure out how to make the show even better. It's an important part of our culture, training and mind set: 'Hang-in-there' until we get it the way we want it— until the show works. 'Hang-in-there' until both team and audience are walking out the door exclaiming, 'I GOT WOWED!'"

Dan and Byron got it. They had experienced the "hang-in-there" mind set the other night. Working through the great moments to make the show work, they had walked out the door saying, "WOW!"

Dan wrote "I Got WOWed!" on his yellow pad. He wanted to remember this nugget. It was the name of the game!

"There you have it," Alex concluded, "a look from behind the eyes of a Flying Trapeze Buddy. Now it's time to see what you can do with this concept back in your business and the rehab center."

The two students nodded politely. It was time to move from theory to action.

> "Courage is grace under pressure."
> – *Ernest Hemingway*

Chapter Seven
The Trapeze Buddy Concept Explained

Enthusiasm screamed from Dan's being as he attempted to explain his weekend activities and business transforming discovery to his executive assistant.

Nathalie sat forward on her chair, trying to keep up with the many segments, tangents and sidebar thoughts presented by her boss.

"I was swinging from a trapeze this weekend and discovered a key to success here at BoMar," explained the CEO. "Well, I didn't find the solution *on* the trapeze itself, but the experience gave me the insight I think we need to move this place to the next level."

Nathalie nodded her head in polite, confused understanding.

Dan reminded Nathalie of a balloon that had been inflated to maximum capacity, then released in the room. He was all over the place.

The excited CEO continued, "Byron, the young man from the Spinal Cord Rehab Center, where I volunteer every month, helped me flesh out and fine tune some of the ideas and strategies. He and his wheel chair buddies clarified several important issues."

Dan drew in a much needed breath. He pondered a brief moment, then added, "And to see those guys and gals leave their wheel chairs and fly from their trapeze was inspiring. Absolutely inspiring. And that serves as the key to our company culture overhaul," Dan concluded.

As he rapidly drew in the next breath, Nathalie sensed her opportunity and jumped in. "Wait a minute! You mean to tell me that by swinging from a trapeze with guys who are in wheelchairs, you've discovered a clue for making BoMar more competitive? Perhaps I missed something, but I just don't get it. Oh, and one more thing," continued the supportive yet questioning assistant, "is this trapeze thing something you do on a regular basis?"

Dan resumed his explanation with renewed vigor. "No, I don't fly on the trapeze on a regular basis. It was a new activity, which produced a massive breakthrough for me and the folks at the rehab center. And no, I didn't wear the fancy tights," Dan offered in anticipation of her next question.

The Trapeze Buddy Success Strategy

He continued, "This Trapeze Buddy thing is the perfect analogy for every person in our company. I sat there watching these guys perform. One person would climb the long ladder to the top of the pole, grab the trapeze bar, then swing to the middle and spin—hoping what would happen?"

Nathalie picked up on the question and quickly answered, "Someone would swing out and catch him?"

"Exactly," commended the CEO. "At a predetermined, agreed upon time, someone from the other side would swing out and catch this guy."

Dan demonstrated the concept by playing both trapeze artists. First, he climbed and climbed his pretend ladder, then grabbed the imaginary trapeze. He then took small little sliding steps across the floor as if he were flying across on his trapeze. He swung his arms in the air to symbolize the spinning process.

Nathalie watched with mild amusement. Suddenly Dan shifted to the role of the catching trapeze artist. From the opposite side he quickly stepped to catch the imaginary spinning trapeze partner. He had to be a secure, confident CEO to be willing to ham it up in order to reinforce a concept.

Dan picked up the dialogue where he had paused, "And what a perfect analogy for every person in our company. Imagine, Nathalie, you climb the ladder, grab the trapeze, swing out to the center and spin. Hoping what is going to happen to you?"

Nathalie was beginning to understand her role in this game, so she answered again, "Someone would swing out and catch me?"

"Exactly," reinforced Dan as he repeated the miniature trapeze artist act. "At a predetermined, agreed upon time, someone from over here would swing out and catch you."

Nathalie nodded her relief in being caught by the imaginary trapeze partner.

But Dan wasn't finished. He rapidly continued, "But how many times have you climbed? You go out to the center, you spin…"

Offering a dramatic pause, Dan slowly walked back to the side of the room where Nathalie's imaginary trapeze partner would be standing. He examined his fingernails and spoke as the phantom trapeze partner: "'Oh, I wanted to be there for her. I thought we could get the project done as promised. I was certain the report would get to her on time.' Or how about these classics: 'The computer system went down, the shipment was delayed, and it's not my job! There's no way I can come through as promised.'" Dan chuckled to himself in amusement, impressed with the aptitude of his metaphor.

"And what's happening to you in the meantime?" asked Dan.

Nathalie sat there, totally engrossed in the message. "I guess I'm still spinning and probably headed for a fall. I hope the safety net is working."

Dan was ready to deliver the punch line for his attentive, one-person audience. "You're right. You're heading for a fall. Put your hands like this," directed Dan. He held his hands about as far apart as he could manage, looking as if he was getting ready to clap. "You're falling, falling, falling and suddenly what happens?" He counted, "One, two, three, SPLAT!" Dan sharply clapped his hands together.

Nathalie caught herself following his lead, "One, two, three, SPLAT!"

Dan now shifted his mood from jocular to serious. "And the sad news is this: there are NO safety nets in our business!" He permitted the idea to sink in.

"In fact, in our business there are spikes sticking up out of the ground! Most people are walking around our company with severe 'spike marks' because one more time, someone they were counting on didn't come through. They got dropped and landed face first on the concrete."

By this time Nathalie was fully engaged, nodding her understanding of and agreement to both the concept and the consequences. She stood to offer her insight. "I know exactly what you mean. I spend 80% of my time trying to track down people who promised to get me information so I can do my job. And I spend the other 60% trying to recover from all the times people just don't come through." She looked at her fingers as if checking the math. Dan clearly understood her meaning.

Nathalie wasn't quite finished with her insight. "It's as if everyone shows up to work with olive oil on their hands. Wouldn't it be amazing if everyone came to work with Velcro instead?"

"Bingo! Right on! Home run! You've got it! That's the million dollar answer," encouraged Dan. "Is that your final answer?" he grinned. Nathalie responded with a confident, "Final answer." The two chuckled.

Both stood silently, allowing the significance of this moment to sink in. On a larger scale, they were both processing what this new model could mean for co-workers, customers, and vendors. The Trapeze Buddy model could even have a positive impact in homes and relationships.

After a few moments, Nathalie offered, "Caught more and dropped less. I like the sound of the concept. And boy, would my life be easier if people simply did what they said they'd do—in the manner they promised it would be done. I like the concept a bunch. How do we get started?"

Dan expanded upon Nathalie's key insight, "Caught more and dropped less by the people you count on most. I see a theme beginning to develop."

"I'm all ears and ready to go," Nathalie exclaimed as she found her chair while grabbing a yellow pad in order to capture the nuggets.

Dan paused to collect his thoughts and mentally map out his game plan. He began, "The Trapeze Buddy concept is quite simple to comprehend. People seem to quickly understand the ramifications of coming through and being caught more often."

"And I quickly understood the ramifications of *not* coming through. I've been spending a lot of time going SPLAT!" interjected Nathalie while clapping both hands.

The training continued, "Our first step is to introduce the Trapeze Buddy concept."

Nathalie wrote: "1. Introduce the concept. People will get it." She looked back up at Dan for the next nugget.

"The second step is the creation of a common definition. We need to be on the same page with this metaphor."

Nathalie asked, "Do you have a common 'Trapeze Buddy' definition in mind?"

"Absolutely," answered Dan. "Byron was a great help. Here's our working definition." He recited the Trapeze Buddy definition while Nathalie captured the idea word for word.

"Let me read it back to you and make sure I've got it," she requested.
> "A Trapeze Buddy is anyone you count on or rely upon to complete a task, a function, or provide you with information so you can get your job done. It's also anyone who counts on *you* to complete a task, function or provide them with information so they can get their job done.

Did I get it?"

"Got it word for word," offered the CEO. "You're pretty quick with that pencil."

"Thanks, I'll take that as a compliment. I have years of practice of trying to keep up with CEO's who are all over the room with a thousand and one thoughts and ideas." Dan nodded his understanding.

"In short," Nathalie stated, "the working definition could be boiled down to this idea: I count on you; you count on me; therefore we're Trapeze Buddies."
Dan appreciated Nathalie's participation in the process. "What else?" Dan inquired.

Nathalie reviewed her yellow pad: "First, introduce the concept. And in order to make it both relevant and fun, I think you'd look superb in tights as you explain the concept to the entire company. I think a powder blue would bring out the color in your eyes."

Dan refused to be baited this time. He simply stared back at the comedienne and smiled.

She returned the smile and continued, "Second, I've recorded a common definition captured in the idea: 'You count on me; I count on you; therefore we're Trapeze Buddies.' What's next?"

Dan jumped in with his explanation of 'Mind Mapping'—creating a detailed list of all Trapeze

Buddies on paper so you can see the magnitude of the interdependent relationships. Moving the concept from your head to a piece of paper—it's that simple.

Nathalie grabbed a separate sheet of paper, placed a quarter sized circle in the middle and wrote her name. She then drew eight similar circles around the circle which had her name on it, thus creating a planet with eight moons circling it.

In one concentric circle she wrote the name of the receptionist, Joan. "If I understand the mind mapping idea correctly," Nathalie inquired, "Joan is a Trapeze Buddy. I'm counting on her to handle the phones and get me the necessary calls."

"Yes," Dan affirmed.

Nathalie drew a line connecting her circle with that of her Trapeze Buddy, Joan. She admired her handiwork, then added an arrowhead on both ends of the line.

The Trapeze Buddy Success Strategy

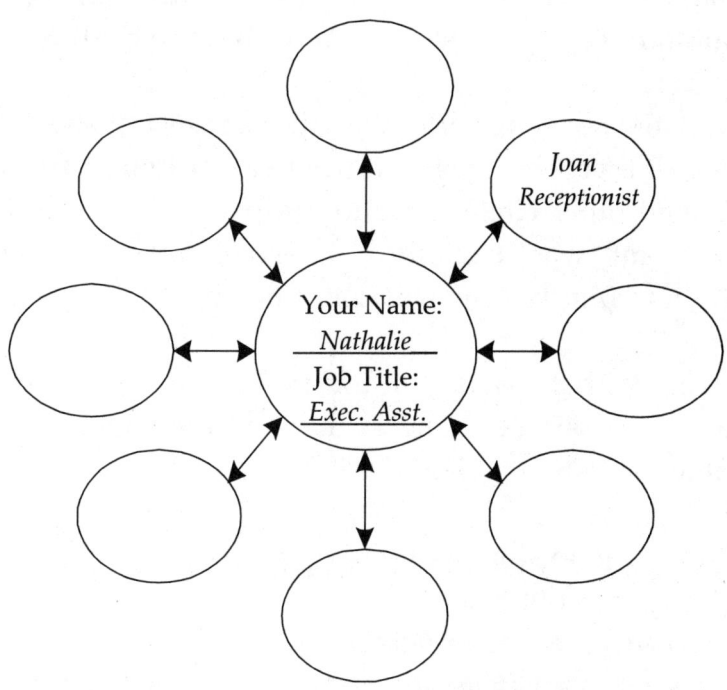

Viewing her creation, Dan inquired, "Tell me about those arrows."

"Well, in this model I know I count on Joan, so I drew an arrow from me to her. But it also occurred to me that she counts on me so she can handle her job effectively. It's consistent with our definition of Trapeze Buddies; we count on each other to get our jobs done. The arrows going in both directions symbolize our interdependence.

Dan was excited by this new piece of the puzzle being put into place. He encouraged Nathalie to continue.

Nathalie began to fill in the other circles but she soon found that her diagram needed additions, so she created other circles around the page. The Executive Assistant was beginning to recognize the many Trapeze Buddies she was counting on every day.

"I think that's about it for now. It's a good start anyway," said Nathalie as she laid the tablet on the table for Dan to review.

Dan began to scan her mind mapping list:
- Receptionist
- Copier repair person
- The seven leaders from the Leadership Team
- The executive assistants for each of the seven leaders
- Dan
- Marketing department
- Janitorial team
- Accounting
- Payroll company
- Human resources
- The manufacturing team
- Customers
- Vendors
- Her family
- Phone system people

- Computer, IS team

Nathalie had jotted down 54 names in two minutes. "Quite a list in such a short period of time," commended Dan. "What do you notice about the list and this activity?"

"Well, I seem to have plenty of Trapeze Buddies," she reflected, adding two more names to the list— limo service and airlines. "It suggests that I'll be noticing many more Trapeze Buddies as I progress through my day.

"One more thing," observed Nathalie. "There are plenty of opportunities to be forsaken during a normal business week. Ouch! No wonder I spend so much time going..." They both spread their arms and clapped at the same time, "SPLAT!"

"That makes it pretty urgent," Dan interjected. "We need to figure out a way to get everyone on the same page—and fast! To use your words, we need to be 'caught more and dropped less by the people we count on most.'"

Both partners suddenly understood the urgency of the matter.

"So where do we go after 'Mind Mapping'?" inquired an eager student.

The Trapeze Buddy Success Strategy

The CEO turned instructor resumed his teaching demeanor. He instructed Nathalie to place a star next to her top three to five most important Trapeze Buddies.

"Admittedly, I can hear the little voices saying, 'But they're all important!'" he offered in a playful manner, "but for this step simply place a star next to the three to five you can identify as your most important Trapeze Buddies."

Nathalie stared at him with a puzzled "Tell me more" look on her face.

"Most important could mean that you interact with your Trapeze Buddy repeatedly. It could also mean that if he drops you, it REALLY hurts—and takes a long time to clean up the mess. Does that explanation help?"

Nathalie nodded and began to review her list. She placed four stars next to important Trapeze Buddies and took a deep breath, "Most important has to include the boss doesn't it?"

"I'd say you'd better put two stars next to his name."

Nathalie smiled and looked up for the next set of instructions.

Suddenly the phone rang—the *Hot line*, a number given only to a select few—Dan's most important Trapeze Buddies.

"Great morning, this is Dan," answered the CEO. He listened intently before responding. "It doesn't sound good. Give me ten minutes to dig into this and I'll call you back personally. Sit by your phone; I'm going to don my Superman outfit and see what we can do. How does that sound?" He listened for a response. "Thanks, I'll call you back in ten."

"Well, back to the real world. Seems that one of our largest clients has been dropped by us—again. And they're sure not happy about it. We'll pick up our discussion later. Any idea where I put my red Superman cape? Please get me Scott in shipping on the phone immediately."

Nathalie could see that Dan was quickly moving into high fix-it gear. She picked up her notes and headed for the phone in an effort to support her Trapeze Buddy.

Dan started the countdown timer on his watch. When he said ten minutes, he meant ten minutes!

"A professional is a person who can do his best at a time when he doesn't particularly feel like it."
— *Alistair Cooke*

CHAPTER EIGHT
The Trapeze Buddy Report Card

The time bomb continued ticking. Dan looked down at the countdown timer on his stopwatch. One minute 53 seconds remaining and counting down. It was time to call the upset client as promised.

"Well, at least you're 'B.Y.W.' on your agreement to call me back," the client and now respected friend and fellow CEO, Linda Johns commented.

Dan offered an explanation of the problem and what was being done to rectify the situation. He included a sincere apology and thanked the client for bringing the issue to his attention.

"You're welcome—and I'm impressed," stated Linda.

The word "impressed" caught Dan off guard, especially in light of the major blunder by his company. Furthermore, he knew that BoMar was on shaky ground, for the competition was knocking at the front door of this important client.

"Impressed?" Dan fed the compliment back to Linda, attempting to gain clarity.

"Yes, impressed. First, you called me back in the time frame you promised. That's unheard of in today's marketplace. Second, you figured out a way to turn the situation around, fast. Third, you explained what you're going to do to prevent it from happening again. And fourth, I picked up on your sincere desire to make things right. I didn't sense I was a bother or a pain in the back end."

Linda allowed her words to sink in before adding, "Seems as if my 'B.Y.W.' comment took hold from our first meeting. I'm glad to see its positive impact. Now, if you could just get the rest of your company to operate from the 'B.Y.W.' standard, you'd be off and running."

The reality of the comment hit Dan like a blow to the solar plexus. If there was one priority on his agenda, it was to coach his people on coming through as promised. "Caught more, dropped less," he thought to himself.

"B.Y.W," repeated Dan. "Be Your Word, that's exactly what we're attempting to do here! But I've got to admit, one CEO to another, it's easier said than done."

"You're absolutely correct about the challenge," replied Linda, "but it's an important topic on every client's 'customer report card.'"

Dan caught himself capturing the words 'customer report card' on his yellow pad. He thought back to the time in Linda's office when she dropped the letters 'B.Y.W.' in his lap, allowing him to mull over the meaning. Feeling like the mouse being played with by a cat, he had to ask, "Customer report card? Tell me more."

"I thought you'd never ask. I was holding my breath to see where you'd go with that tidbit," she smirked.

"Well, the B.Y.W. stuff was extremely profound, so I figure this customer report card thing must have some merit."

As she explained the "customer report card" theory to Dan, he made several notes on the key points. Each customer has a report card, complete with "how to win with me" criteria. "Our job is to determine what's on his report card and score an 'A' or 100% every time. If we do this, we earn the right to do more business with said customer," finished Linda.

Dan understood the concept but admitted that he had never formalized it in such an easy-to-understand fashion.

He braved a question of his client, "So, if every one of my clients has a 'customer report card,' I need to figure out the scoring criteria they're using to evaluate my company's performance?"

"Correct. Go on."

"Then it's our job to determine what's on your report card regarding our company?"

"Makes good business sense to me," she affirmed.

Dan kept moving forward in his quest for clarity. "So what exactly is on the report you're holding to evaluate our performance?"

"That's the six million dollar question," Linda responded. "One that must wait until another time. I'm late for a meeting and must get back to the people who were impacted by the breakdown today. But I welcome the conversation. It's a win-win topic. After all, how can you hit a target you can't see?"

Linda knew she had just dropped another nugget into Dan's lap. He'd be processing this gem for several moments. She was exactly right, for Dan was feverishly scratching, "How can we hit a target we can't see?" on his yellow pad.

"Got to run," said the client, "but let's discuss the items on my report card soon." And in a flash she was gone.

Dan looked at his notes, reviewing the whirlwind conversation. He took a deep breath. Perhaps this could be a great moment if he could transfer the key learnings to his team and apply the insights to the Trapeze Buddy model.

While dining with his family, the customer report card began to take form. As he reviewed the highlights of the day with his wife, son and chocolate Labrador retriever, the trio listened patiently. They knew that their job was to serve as a supportive sounding board while the CEO, now turned husband, father and dog lover, performed his nightly download.

When he explained the Trapeze Buddy concept, everyone seemed to understand the point. He continued with the "report card" theory, asking his wife to reveal the important items on her report card. Earlier in the day, Dan had placed a large star next to his wife's name. Very smart—a politically correct move on his part!

Dan's wife offered several insights, enough to get the idea ball rolling. Dan picked up a few ideas from another important Trapeze Buddy, his son. The dog just listened politely, groaned and rolled over. As a canine, he was always a good sounding board but limited on ideas and positive input.

At the office the following morning, Dan was excited to try out the customer report card concept with Nathalie. He wanted to determine its relevance to their clients and the Trapeze Buddy model. She grabbed her yellow pad and headed for his office.

"You remember the not-so-happy-call from the client yesterday?" asked Dan.

"Yes."

"One ray of sunshine from the call arrived in the 'Customer Report Card' concept." Dan checked to make sure his assistant was with him. She nodded. "Basically, every client, customer or guest has a 'score card' evaluating our performance. If we score an 'A' on the topics important to them, we earn the right to keep their business. Score an 'F' and we lose their business to the competition."

Nathalie chimed in, "Probably doesn't even need to be an 'F' to lose the business. Keep scoring 'C's' and you're probably out the door in today's competitive environment."

Nathalie's insight and participation fueled Dan's excitement. The two were once again on the same page.

"Exactly!" responded the now supercharged CEO. "And I submit that our Trapeze Buddies also have mental report cards evaluating **our** performance."

"Go on!" Nathalie encouraged.

"Last night I discovered an important Trapeze Buddy in my universe—my wife. She has a mental report card that reads at the top, 'This is how I know Dan loves me.' If I score an 'A' on the items most important to her, where do I get to sleep?" asked Dan, waiting for the predictable answer.

"Indoors?" offered Nathalie.

"Very funny—but accurate," retaliated Dan. "Actually, the more I think about it, the more you're right on target. I get to sleep inside the house!"

Dan continued with his explanation of the Trapeze Buddy Report card. "I'm certain that several items are important to my wife. The first item on her 'This is how I know Dan loves me' report card is that she wants to be told—and told often—that I love her, care for her, appreciate her. And, help me from a lady's perspective, do I need to say it just right?"

"Absolutely!"

Dan mused, "You're right. It does me no good to walk in the door and mutter, 'Love you' in a monotone grunt. It just doesn't work. The words were right, but the feeling wasn't there."

A chuckle of understanding and agreement expelled from Nathalie's side of the room.

"The second item on my wife's, 'This is how I know Dan loves me scorecard,' is that she likes to be held. She wants me to touch her, hold her and hug her. And again, help me out here," gesturing toward his assistant, "do I need to hold her just right?"

An affirmative head nod confirmed the answer.

Dan was now moving full swing into his example and beginning to ham it up a bit. "I've found it doesn't work," he explained, "to enter the house and do my 'Super-strong-man' routine, breaking four of her ribs while passionately squeezing her." Dan demonstrated his "Super-strong-man" routine with an intense flex soliciting another chuckle from his audience.

"The third thing on my wife's report card," expounded Dan, "is the fact that she loves me to buy her small, expensive gifts."

Relating to the "small expensive gifts" concept, Nathalie anticipated the next illustration.

Dan proceeded, "So does it work anymore when I go away on a business trip, and return with the shower cap from the Holiday Inn in Omaha for her?"

A "no way" headshake confirmed the answer.

"You're right! It doesn't work anymore!" remarked Dan. "The shower cap was effective during our first two years of marriage, but now, it just doesn't cut it.

So if I'm masterful at doing the things important to her—on the 'this is how I know Dan loves me' report card—who wins?"

Nathalie pondered the question for a moment.

Her thoughts were interrupted by Dan's hurried comment, "You're probably thinking, 'It really depends on how expensive the little gift was.' Am I right?" he asked.

The two chuckled.

"You're right," responded Nathalie, "expense was a major consideration. Bottom line—an excellent report card creates a win-win relationship."

Nathalie expanded, "I know that when my husband takes the time to make sure my report card is in great shape, I'm much more willing and motivated to take good care of him. Without a doubt we both win."

The CEO was pleased that his illustration had hit the mark. He continued, "So, Nathalie, if our spouses fashion mental report cards, would it make sense that our other important Trapeze Buddies also create them?"

"I don't see why not. Yet I know I've never sat down with a business Trapeze Buddy and attempted to see what was most important to him."

"Exactly!" exclaimed the CEO. "We don't ask, so we don't know. We assume that we know what works for them, but judging by the results, we're off base many times. How can I assume we're off base? Because we spend a lot of time going SPLAT! So I ask you, how can we hit a target we can not see?"

Nathalie pondered the depth of his question, then remarked with an impressed smile, "Dan, you're getting pretty philosophical, aren't you?"

"Yeah, I know, pretty deep, isn't it?" he chuckled. "But our upset client offered me the nugget yesterday. We assume that we know what's important to her and her company, but when was the last time we asked? It's like cramming for a test—you know the material perfectly only to discover that you've studied the wrong subject. Ouch."

"So let's take it a step further," began Nathalie. "You had me mind map all my Trapeze Buddies, and I placed a star next to the most important ones. Would the next step be for me to develop a Trapeze Buddy Report Card with my most important partners?"

Dan was intrigued by this line of discovery. He encouraged her to continue.

"Well," explained the assistant, "it's beginning to make sense. If I have a conversation with you and ask, 'What do you need from ME in order to do your job brilliantly?' the likelihood of hitting the target you mentioned is greatly enhanced. It seems we'd be caught more and dropped less, and that's our objective."

The big picture was beginning to emerge for Nathalie. "And it'd be to your advantage to ask me what I need from you in order to do my job brilliantly. It's part of creating a win-win relationship."

"Right on target," affirmed the CEO. "We'd know exactly how to win with each other, and the positive outcome promises fewer trips to the concrete—or the spikes."

"If we take it a step further and asked each of our key clients how to win with them, I'll bet we would hit the bull's-eye much more consistently."

The CEO liked what he heard from his assistant. "Create a Trapeze Buddy Report Card with all our key Trapeze Buddies, hit the bull's-eye more often, and be caught more and dropped less. Perfect."

Dan pondered the concept. Then he asked, "So what would go on those Trapeze Buddy Report Cards?"

Before she could answer, Dan's next appointment appeared at the door.

"Knock, knock," announced Barry, head of IT. "Am I at the right place at the right time?"

"Perfect timing, Barry. It couldn't have been better," confirmed the CEO. "We were just discussing the Trapeze Buddy Report Card concept. Let me ask you, what are the important items on your Trapeze Buddy Report Card?"

Offering his "deer in the headlights" stare, Barry had no clue what the CEO had just asked him.

Dan smiled, then gently added, "Don't worry, we'll explain the concept in detail. Come in and have a seat. I've been looking forward to chatting with you."

The Trapeze Buddy Success Strategy

"The secret to success with people: Give them more of what motivates them and less of what irritates them."
— *Mark Rosenberger*

CHAPTER NINE
Trapeze Buddy Distinctions

T ap, tap, tap. Cold, flannel-gray rain rhythmically used Dan's head as a snare drum. Click, click, click. Dan's impatient toe tapped in a saran wrap thin layer of water. His limo driver was late—again. They would be rushing frantically to the airport—again. It would be tight getting through the check-in line, past security and onto the plane. Again.

Dan's go-getter instinct was feeling hampered. One more time he had been "dropped" by someone he was counting on. "And to think Nathalie phoned these clowns to remind them of my trip today," he groaned. He looked at his watch for the 42nd time in the last two minutes. The toe tapping quickened. Dan was visibly irritated.

As he reached for his cell phone, a car screeched around the corner and came to a skidding halt on the slick pavement. Out leaped a well-groomed gentleman in his mid sixties who hustled to the passenger side of the car. "I'm sorry I'm late. I can't believe it. I'm late, and I hate being late," he apologized as he held the passenger door open for Dan.

As the door closed, the remorse-filled driver hastened back to his driver's seat and turned to address his passenger. "I'm sorry I'm late. This is not a good start on my first REAL day on the job. I'm sincerely sorry for being late." The driver made sure the apology had been heard, then continued, "Allow me to introduce myself—my name is Darrell. It'll be my pleasure to be of service—now that I've found you."

Acknowledging the driver's apology, Dan asked the distinguished looking, sun tanned driver to make a beeline for the airport. "You drive, and we can discuss this situation on the way," directed an impatient CEO. "First REAL day on the job," thought Dan. "Why me?"

As the town car rolled toward its destination, Dan sat back and took in a long, deep breath. He exhaled with slow deliberation as if blowing out all of the tension from the day. He yielded a grin, reflecting on the Sesame Street character teaching his young son to "breathe in the good and breathe out the bad." "Keep breathing," remembered Dan. "Stop for more than about 5 minutes and it can really wreck your day." With the tension released, Dan turned his attention to the anxious driver.

"First REAL day on the job," said Dan, offering special emphasis to the word REAL. "How many days total have you been with this company, Darrell?"

"Three days," offered the driver with a hint of concern in his voice. "I recognize it's not a great way to get started by being late for one of my best customers."

Dan was impressed by Darrell's sincere desire to do right, to take care of the customer. But he was not impressed with the delivery of service. The driver was late, pure and simple. Dan decided to explore further. "Three days, that's all?" asked Dan with an inquisitive tone. "You really are a rookie with this company. What did you do the first two days on the job?"

Thinking for a moment before responding, Darrell answered, "The first day I sat through the most boring session of my life. We sifted through tons of paper work, endured a safety lecture and basically experienced another chauffeur's class. The class was presented by the most monotonous humdrum, lifeless speaker in the universe. He basically placed overheads on the projection unit with print so small I couldn't read it from ten feet away. Then he read the pages word for word!" The driver voiced a high degree of agony in recalling the painful experience. There was no tone of blame, only painful regret.

"Ouch," empathized Dan, "that's pretty painful stuff. Did you at least have good donuts to eat during the slow and agonizing death?"

"You know, we were never offered donuts. The instructor told us that they once served donuts during the safety session, but now they were looking for ways to save money. I think they save even more on the nasty coffee they serve during the day." He continued with a mild attempt at humor, "You let coffee sit out for a day or two, then dilute it with some hot water, you can make it last a long time."

"Pretty nasty," agreed Dan. "Tell me about your second day on the job."

"The second day was less painful, but then again, a root canal would have been less painful after day one. Day two can best be described as information overload. We were given files with the names of over 125 key accounts. The files were complete with company name, address, usual passenger names, directions to the business and specific billing instructions. It was our job to 'know the customers.' We then received a half hour lecture on 'good customer service.' It was a lot crammed down our throat, and quite frankly, I don't feel that I was set up to win."

"Set up to win?" questioned Dan. "What do you mean by that?" Dan had often used the phrase himself.

"Well, 'set up to win' means I'm given the information and skill sets I need to win on the job. I'm set up to perform my job brilliantly, and as a result, I can take great care of you, my customer."

Darrell was beginning to reveal his experience and expertise. This was not his first "trip around the block" and his graying hair lent added credibility to his wit and wisdom. He allowed the explanation to sink in, then broke the brief silence with a question, "Are you really interested in this 'set-up to win' discussion, or should I just be quiet and drive?"

Dan was deep in thought, recalling his own first day on the job orientation class. He had to acknowledge that "set-up to win" was not accomplished during his class. As Dan processed the driver's question, he straightened himself, adding, "No, this is great. I love this stuff. Do you have more?"

"Allow me to give you one 'set-up to win' example," the driver continued. "As the new hire, you'd think they'd want to give me pretty good instructions on how to get to your office, don't you think?"

"Sure," responded Dan. "Seems like a basic fundamental for a new hire."

"I was late because the instructions they gave me were perfect except for two little streets missing from the directions. When I made it to the ocean, I knew something was wrong. However, there are no maps in the car. No Thomas Brother's guide, no maps, no navigation system. I would have brought my own Thomas Brother's Street guide, but they told us that every car was equipped with a map under the driver's seat. I found no map under this seat, the passenger seat or your seat," explained a frustrated driver, pointing to the rear seats.

It was obvious that Darrell did not like being set up to lose. It appeared that he had been "dropped" by the person providing the directions and equipping the car. Ouch, and now Dan had been dropped and was running late for his flight.

The driver's explanation continued. "And to make matters worse, when I realized I was lost and most likely would be late, I called the office for clarity on the driving directions. After all, I'm not the first person who has ever driven to your office. Would you believe that they put me on hold for seven minutes? I drove in circles for seven minutes before someone could help me figure out what was wrong with the directions. It was extremely painful. If I owned the company, you can be assured there would be some major changes."

The Trapeze Buddy Success Strategy

Dan was experiencing flashbacks to an earlier breakdown with one of his important customers. It was the predictable pattern: people not coming through as promised. He had spent too much time cleaning up the mess. Now he was sitting in the back of a town car on his way to the airport, the victim of people not coming through. "Pretty painful," he offered back to Darrell in agreement.

Intuition told Dan he needed to learn more from the limo driver. He obviously had a perspective from the front seat which Dan lacked from the back seat, as well as years of practical experience under his belt.

"So what could the company have done to set you up to win from day one?" ventured Dan, knowing they still had a considerable drive to the airport.

Darrell was beginning to enjoy the conversation, sensing that Dan was genuinely interested in his situation and the process of moving performance to the next level. "First, I think it's more a matter of distinctions." The driver allowed the word "distinctions" to take on added emphasis. "Distinctions describe the attitudes and behaviors needed to play successfully on this limo team," he concluded.

Dan sat straight up in his seat, sensing a new insight in the making. He encouraged the driver to dig deeper. "Go on."

"The company gave us the thirty minute 'Good Service' lecture. Good service could mean one thing to me, paint an entirely different picture for another new driver and still another picture for you, the customer. Distinctions help us clarify what good service means so everyone is on the same page. If we're all on the same page from day one, the likelihood of hitting the good service bull's-eye is greatly enhanced," explained the driver, now turned distinction expert. He obviously had given this situation serious thought and consideration before working with his new company.

"So how do distinctions help in the process?" asked Dan.

The driver was ready for the question and eager to explain further. "Think of it this way. Have you ever experienced 'bad' service from another company?"

"Why certainly. In fact, I suspect that I am often selected to win bad service from numerous companies," Dan offered with an ironic grin on his face.

"Perfect," continued the distinction expert. "Let's pick one of the latest episodes in which you've received bad service. And please pick an experience other than my being late with you today."

Dan caught the driver's eyes and played along. "Got one, and it's not your being late today."

"Perfect," coached the driver. "Now let's evaluate the attitudes and behaviors of the person providing you the service. Can you describe some of those attitudes and behaviors evident during the service breakdown—and you can't simply use the word 'bad'; you must dig deeper." The driver waited to see if his request had registered with Dan.

"For example, the waiter was 'rude,'" offered Dan. "Would that be a 'bad' attitude or behavior for this exercise?"

"Exactly. Few people would place 'rude' on the positive side of the distinction list. What else?"

Beginning to get the flow of the game, Dan thought back to his "bad service" experience. "Let's see," he began, "he didn't listen, acted like it was my fault the dinner was lousy, didn't care, argued with me, gave me the run around, and then ignored me."

By now, Dan was fully reliving his painful service experience. Darrell heard the sharp tone in Dan's voice and noticed the veins beginning to bulge and pulsate in his neck. "And they acted like non-thinking robots," offered Dan in a final volley of disdain and disgust. "There, how'd I do?"

"And they were 'rude'!" reminded Darrell.

"Right!" returned Dan's voice with an added edge, "they were REALLY rude! Keep breathing. One, two, three." Dan counted aloud as he reminded himself to "breathe in the good and breathe out the bad." He never realized that Sesame Street would become so beneficial to his emotional and physical well being.

Darrell was eager to continue the lesson. "So now we have a list of 'bad' service distinctions—words which describe the attitudes and behaviors of how NOT to provide service. By the way, do you feel that you need to tell me the entire story of your bad service experience? You seem pretty worked up."

Dan's belly deep, bass drum chuckle shifted the entire mood of the car. "No, it'd take too long to explain all my problems from early childhood." The CEO gained his composure saying, "Back to our list of 'bad service' distinctions. How does that list set you up to win on your job?"

"Thanks for asking," replied the driver, who knew his class would end at the airport and wanted to put one or two pieces of the puzzle into place before the trip was over. "We want to create distinctions to provide 'good service,' transforming the negative list into a positive list—bad distinctions into good distinctions."

Dan quickly jumped into the line of thought. "So if I reconstructed my restaurant experience and coached the staff on how to take good care of me, I'd come up with a different set of words—a different set of positive distinctions."

"Bingo!" offered the proud instructor. "Give it a shot."

Dan was now ready to venture an opinion. "First, I'd change the word 'rude' to 'polite' or 'considerate.' I'd then coach the restaurant staff to communicate with me, be solution oriented, fix the problem quickly, listen, and take ownership in the situation and the solution." Dan paused a moment before continuing. "I'd coach the staff to be proactive and take pride in the goal of having every single customer walk out the door saying, 'I Got WOWed!'"

"You've got it," cheered the driver. "So how might those distinctions help you set up a new employee in your company to win from day one?" He wanted to connect the dots between concept and application, knowing that Dan was now ready to answer his earlier question about the benefits of distinctions.

Dan looked out the window at the traffic zipping past. He discovered the connection—coach people how to win at our company. He saw "distinctions" as words which describe the specific attitudes and behaviors needed to win on his team. Dan could coach and demonstrate what "polite" might look like at his company. He could describe, outline, coach, measure and reinforce *effective communication* in his company. He could use distinctions to take all the guesswork out of what it means to win at BoMar Industries. He could explain to new hires on their first day the specific attitudes and behaviors needed to win at BoMar. Dan now had a model for his new Trapeze Buddies. He called it "Success Characteristics," the attitudes and behaviors needed by all Trapeze Buddies to be caught more and dropped less by the people they count on most.

As the car pulled up to the curb at United Airlines and glided to a landing along side the curb, Darrell dashed around to assist his passenger.

"It was a very enlightening ride to the airport," Dan concluded as he extended his hand to Darrell. "Thanks. I appreciate your desire to win and your penetrating insights."

The driver modestly nodded. "Thank you for both compliments. The discussion was fun for me as well."

As Dan turned to depart, he paused momentarily and then asked, "By the way, I sense this is not the first time you've had a discussion about distinctions and how to improve team performance. What's your background?"

"I'm retired. I drive this limo only one day a week—it helps keep my pulse on the real world. Plus I get to meet interesting people like you." Darrell explained further, "The rest of my week includes two or three rounds of golf, at least one date-day with my bride and the rest of the time is consumed with volunteer projects, family events and planning my next career."

"What did you retire from?"

"Most recently I was the CEO for a large manufacturing company. Lots of people, plenty of challenges and loads of rewards."

Dan stared in disbelief. He allowed the driver's answer to bounce around in his head for a moment. "A retired CEO? I knew it! There was something about this conversation and your authority on the subject that made me sit-up and take notice."

Darrel grinned with the satisfaction of knowing his well kept secret had been revealed to a worthy student. He also sensed this would not be the last time the two CEO's shared ideas, techniques and strategies.

Before long Dan settled into his airplane seat, jotting insights on his yellow pad. One more time, valuable insights had come from the most unlikely source. And from another CEO. Quite fascinating!

CHAPTER TEN
Trapeze Buddies Success Characteristics

"One, two three, Splat!" chanted an enthusiastic CEO. He spread his arms open as wide as possible and rapidly brought his hands together for a loud clap at the precise moment the group yelled "SPLAT!"

"Again, what happens when someone doesn't come through as promised: one, two, three, SPLAT!" Dan led another energy packed clap.

"What happens when someone moves my trapeze? One, two, three, SPLAT!" Dan and the entire Leadership Team grinned. They understood the concept!

The Leadership Team had spent the day learning about the Trapeze Buddy Model, introduced to the concept by some rather unlikely instructors: Dan discussed the importance of **coming through** as promised; Alex, the REAL life Flying Trapeze Artist, developed the concept via his **C.A.T.C.H.** technology;

Byron, from the Spinal Cord Rehab Center, coached the Leadership Team on the **Mind Mapping** concept; Executive Assistant Nathalie did a spectacular job teaching the team the **Trapeze Buddy Report Card** element. Two other guest instructors helped with the program: Linda Johns, customer and CEO, brought her own unique perspective on **B.Y.W.** and its application to gain a competitive advantage; Darrell, limo driver and retired CEO, shared strategies on **distinctions**.

Dan was impressed by the attentiveness of his Leadership Team throughout the day. They truly wanted to understand the concepts and apply them to their situation. He wondered if they saw the model as a tool for gaining a significant competitive advantage. Perhaps the team members were interested in getting more done with fewer headaches and hassles. They were surely tired of being dropped and landing face down in the concrete. Or, were they anticipating the fact that in less than two hours the entire team would be climbing high above the circus floor for its own trapeze experience? It didn't really matter why as long as they embraced the idea. But the thought of swinging from high above the circus floor did seem to capture their attention. And with all the employees invited to the event, it placed added pressure on this leadership squad.

The team reviewed the key elements:
- The Trapeze Buddy Concept—we're all counting on many people everyday;
- The Trapeze Buddy Definition—I count on you and you count on me, therefore we're Trapeze Buddies;
- The Report Card Concept—customers and Trapeze Buddies walk around with mental score cards;
- The importance of setting people up to win— to be caught more and dropped less by the people they're counting on most!

After the review, Dan needed to install one more piece to the puzzle before he turned the team over to Alex. He wanted them to discover "Success Characteristics" for a new hire at BoMar industries. Who better to lead the discussion than the limo driver and retired CEO who had shared the concepts of distinctions with Dan? Darrell was now on center stage, feeling at home in this environment.

"Let's say I'm the new hire in your department. It's your job to coach me on the three to five critical elements for being an effective Trapeze Buddy at your company. What would I hear?"

The Leadership Team broke into two groups to address the challenge, armed with flip charts and an assortment of colored markers. The instructors for the day divided themselves among the teams to move the process forward. The room became a beehive of activity.

From Byron's wheelchair you could hear the word "Passionate." But then, what would you expect to hear from such a player? "Passionate" was captured on the flip chart.

The entire room heard Nathalie offer, "Thorough, a good listener and timely."

Byron was all over the contribution by Nathalie, "Way to go, Porsche Lady!"

When the group offered a puzzled stare, expecting an explanation, Byron complied. "I call Nathalie the Porsche Lady because she's fast, thorough—and you'd better not get in her way. Just like someone in a speeding Porsche. Get it?" The group responded with "bad joke" moans.

A "good communicator" was identified by one group; "team player" was placed on the other team's flip chart. Dozens of distinctions were added to the various flip charts. Now the teams were instructed to come together, review the lists, and vote for the five most important Trapeze Buddy Success Characteristics for BoMar Industries. Each person was given eight votes and could weight his vote—if he felt particularly strong about one distinction, he could cast all eight votes for the one. A pretty simple process, but it seemed to take a week to distribute all the votes.

At last the voting was complete. The top five vote getters included
- Communication
- Honesty
- Trust
- Flexibility
- Teamwork

Darrell asked the team how they felt about the selection. Group gloat would best describe their satisfaction. They were rather impressed with their accomplishment.

Darrell continued his coaching, "So here's what we're saying: if I'm the new hire at BoMar and can demonstrate these five Success Characteristics on a consistent basis, I'm likely to be an effective Trapeze Buddy?"

The group affirmed its complete agreement.

"And further, we understand that these are the five success characteristics for your company. They might be different at another company or with Alex's team on the real trapeze, for example."

The group nod continued.

"Here's the next step," Darrell added. "I'm the new hire, and I need a brave volunteer to coach me how to win at BoMar. You're going to use the Success Characteristics that you just created. Any brave volunteers?"

The group nod ended. Each person sat silently, hoping another team member would raise his hand. Finally, to the collective sigh of the rest of the team, Barb Moss, Head of Distribution, stepped forward. She received added encouragement from the other participants, who were glad they were spared the exercise.

Barb acknowledged the support of the team with a queenlike wave to her adoring subjects.

"Okay, Darrell, as the new hire at BoMar," Barb began before she was interrupted by Byron rolling forward in his wheel chair.

"I'm a new hire, too," interjected Byron, now sitting next to Darrell.

"Fine, and thank you," continued Barb, skipping just a beat or two because of the interruption. "Now, as I was saying, you two are the new hires at BoMar." But before she could formulate the next sentence on her tongue, Nathalie, as if on cue, raised her hand with an enthusiastic attention getter.

"Hey, how about me? I'm a new hire, too." She assumed her place between Darrell and Byron. "And look," she said, drawing attention to her being between the two men, "a rose among the thorns." Her sheepish smirk sent the exact message she wanted delivered to the men, and she received the appropriate group laugh.

"Well," began Barb for the third time, "I seem to be doing pretty well in my recruiting. Anyone else want to be a new employee?" She shot a penetrating glance toward Dan and Alex.

"Absolutely," came the response from both men in harmony. They took their spots at the front of the room with the other new hires.

"So where was I?" asked Barb. "I think I was welcoming you to BoMar as the new hires. Being an effective Trapeze Buddy is very important to your success with the company and the company's long-term success." Barb was now in full stride in her role as instructor.

"Here are five attitudes and behaviors that will help you win at BoMar," she continued, placing the five distinctions on the flip chart. "Communication,

Honesty, Trust, Flexibility, and Teamwork. There you go; let's be great Trapeze Buddies together."

The five new hires just stood there. No action, no reaction, no expression. They stood perfectly still as if waiting to be instructed to breathe. Barb was uneasy with the pose and asked if there was something more she should do or say.

No response—just a stone faced stare. The new hires seemed to be from a foreign planet, comprehending nothing. When Barb noted that it reminded her of staff meetings, the comment drew laughter from the audience and quick grins from the new hires, who promptly returned to the death stare.

"O.K, team, let's roll," Barb declared for lack of anything better to say.

Darrell then stepped forward from the clump of new hires, announcing, "The new hires will now demonstrate the attitudes and behaviors outlined by this Leadership Team. We'll begin with 'Communication.'"

As if on cue, Byron rolled past the seated Leadership Team to the center of the room. He spun quite effectively in one spot, turning his wheel chair to face his audience. After a dramatic pause, now certain that he had everyone's undivided attention, he let out a monosyllabic grunt. He again paused, smiled and rolled back to his original position.

Nathalie stepped forward as if being handed the baton from Byron. The back of her hand was glued to her forehead, the perfect "victim pose." "You should meet my boss—woe is me," began the impassioned assistant, turned drama queen. "Nobody seems to understand. They're all against me. I'll never get all this work done. Why am **I** the **only** one who seems to be pulling her weight around here?" She thrust herself down in a chair, her head thrown back with extra victim emphasis. "Oh, and by the way, someone called for you today." Nathalie held the dramatic victim pose before standing and walking back to the new hire group, her hand still glued to her forehead.

"A round of applause for the Academy Award winning performance," urged Dan, leading the audience in enthusiastic applause. "And to think," he continued, "you didn't even need to pretend."

The room knew Dan was playfully skating on thin ice with his comment.

Not to be outdone, Nathalie again stepped forward, her hand still glued to her forehead. "Keep those comments coming and you'll not even get your one message. And remember, paybacks can be hell."

Dan humbly acknowledged the comeback; he then assumed his role as new hire and faced the Leadership Team. He began to communicate to the group, but because of his excessive mumbling and irritating array of odd noises, they could understand just about one word in ten. Dan returned to his new hire position on the side of the room.

Next, Alex stepped forward to address the group. "Oh, I forgot to tell you, but about a week ago a customer called. I don't remember which one at the moment, but he wanted to speak with you real bad. Said it was something to do with some kind of problem, but I don't remember what kind of problem. I'm thinking you might want to call him before he gets really upset. Boy, was he mad, yelling stuff like…" At this moment Nathalie walked forward and placed her arm around Alex's shoulder, directing him back to his spot on the side of the room.

"You'll be fine," she offered in an assuring, warm, motherly voice. "We'll get your cookies and milk and everything will be fine."

"Sounds like one of my staff meetings," interjected Tom Murphy, Head of HR, now turned comedian. His efforts paid off with another hearty group laugh. Everyone on the Leadership Team could relate to the comment.

The Trapeze Buddy Success Strategy

Darrell assumed his position in the front of the room, asking the group, "What did you notice about our demonstration?"

Tom Murphy offered, "The skit seemed like a 'put on,' but it also had some real world communication. We get this stuff all the time. Granted, it's usually not so dramatic, but you'd be amazed at the communication going on in our company."

Darrell acknowledged Tom's contribution; he then pointed to Barb, encouraging her to respond. She enthusiastically waved her hand in the air, appearing about ready to pop.

"I now clearly see what effective Trapeze Buddy communication means to me. I also understand it could be very different to other members of the team. The demonstration by our New Hire team suggests that we seriously consider what effective communication means at BoMar. And we'll have to do the same for the other success characteristics as well."

Darrell and Dan offered Barb high-fives. She had hit the nail on the head.

The teams returned to their groups with instructions to take each of the five success characteristics and further identify distinctions which clearly articulated the exact attitudes and behaviors desired at BoMar.

Alex offered an example as a means to "prime the pump" for this important activity. "On the trapeze tonight, timing is going to be a very important key to your success. So if I just tell you 'timing,' it could mean twelve different things to twelve different people. It's my job to clearly articulate what 'timing' means to me and how we use it to succeed together. Otherwise I leave it up to your imagination and past life experiences to figure it out. And here's what will happen," said Alex while spreading his arms for the all-too-familiar SPLAT! clap, "one, two, three, **SPLAT**!" Every person in the room joined in the demonstration.

The groups departed and soon returned with their completed list:

Communication: Concise, clear, to the point, useful, necessary, timely, accurate, kind
Honesty: Sincere, speak your mind, non-political
Trust: Accountable, dependable, discreet, responsible, respectful
Flexible: Open-minded, willing, adaptive, innovative
Teamwork: Cooperative, participative, helpful, supportive, equal/fair

The Trapeze Buddy Success Strategy

Dan assumed his spot in the front of the group. "Excellent effort on your Success Characteristics! Here's our goal: we want to create win-win-win relationships. We want the employees, the customers and the company to win. Basically, we expect all of our Trapeze Buddies to be caught more and dropped less. This is one of the most important pieces to our performance puzzle—setting people up to win! We do this with clear expectations, understanding exactly what each of these words looks like on the job." Dan paused to make sure his points had hit home. The nodding heads verified that the pieces of today's class were coming together.

Dan continued with his closing remarks. "We've all spent way too much time face down in the concrete. The reason: people didn't come through as promised. They thought they had communicated, but they missed one of the important elements." Pointing to the flip chart for added emphasis he continued, "They missed being 'concise,' 'clear,' 'to the point,' 'useful,' 'timely' or 'accurate,' and now we're all paying the price. Tonight you'll be offered a chance to be a real Flying Trapeze Artist under the careful supervision of Alex and his team. Here's my promise: you'll walk away with more insights into this process than I could ever share with you. So get ready to fly. And one more thing, have some fun. We'll be taping tonight's event. See you there."

A strong voice spoke up from the wheelchair on the other side of the room. "If it's any encouragement to you, I flew on the Flying Trapeze! It's safe to say that I have a few more challenges than anyone in this room. If I can do it, you can do it, too." Byron continued like a game show host who had downed a triple espresso before grabbing the mike. "And finally, ladies and gentlemen, we'd like to acknowledge the new star of the Flying Trapeze, a man who will look especially dashing in his new, powder blue, sequin studded Flying Trapeze outfit."

At that precise moment, Alex stepped forward, revealing the powder blue costume for all to behold. On the front, silver sequin letters announced: "Dan, the Flying CEO."

Dan could only shake his head in absolute embarrassment as the group broke into enthusiastic applause and laughter. He reached for Byron's head to offer the familiar, friendly head thump, but the wheels were much too allusive.

Chapter Eleven
The First Big Step

If excitement were a flame, Dan's office would erupt into a forest fire! Last night's BoMar Company Flying Trapeze event was a roaring success.

"Come here and give me a high five," commanded Dan to the giddy Barb Moss, who had the look in her eye of someone who, much to her amazement, had just accomplished the impossible.

She found the outstretched hands of her boss, slapped them and held on. "Thanks, Dan," she began in an emotional release of gratitude. "That was perhaps the biggest breakthrough I've had in my life. I was scared to death! But I kept telling myself to go as far as I could and then take one more step. And, I did it! I did it!" proclaimed Barb as she added some extra squeeze to the high five.

Nathalie entered Dan's office, moving as if she were levitating from one side of the room to another. The look in her eye told the rest of the group the entire message: "AWESOME!"

And so the morning would continue, person after person walking away with an experience that was impossible to put into words but which had rendered a profound impact.

Each employee from BoMar was given the opportunity to rehearse his own Flying Trapeze experience under the masterful coaching of Alex and his team. At the end of the session, Alex selected ten lucky contestants to perform in the Grande Finale show with his troupe. The employees went berserk! Seeing their co-workers "swing through the air with the greatest of ease" was simply too much. The evening was filled with sidesplitting laughter, hand numbing applause and story after story of personal breakthroughs.

"I was ready to swing but someone moved my trapeze," explained a co-worker to Nathalie. "And then it hit me—this is how I feel many days when people don't come through. I kept asking, who moved my trapeze?"

Dan gathered up the Leadership Team and addressed three questions:
    "1. What were the take-a-ways from last night's Flying Trapeze event?

2. How do we bottle this momentum and move it to the next level?
3. How do we move the concepts into our organization?"

Around the room they proceeded, identifying their favorite concepts: facing fear yet moving forward in spite of the fear; clearly understanding the C.A.T.C.H. technology; adopting the Great Moments mentality; identifying the number of times co-workers had been dropped by the Leadership Team; anticipating operation of the company with this level of energy and focus; missing the mark but being willing to try again until achieving success; viewing each person in the organization as a vital piece of the show—no "I'm just a..." jobs; creating a strategy where co-workers could establish a win-win relationship.

Thus the meeting continued with new insights, amazing "ah ha's," useable take-aways, a resounding sense of accomplishment and a renewed sense of hope. For the first time in a long time the group understood that success or failure lay clearly in their hands.

The brainstorming session designed to leverage the momentum was filled with a vast array of possibilities following these important brainstorming guidelines:

1. No wrong answers—just capture ideas because all ideas are valuable;
2. No fire hosing—no one can kill the ember of an idea;
3. Play outside the box, get crazy, have some fun.

Of the usable strategies developed, Dan's favorites included challenging each department to bring the Trapeze Buddy concept to life into its areas of responsibility; preparing a "Flying Trapeze Buddy Handbook" for new hires as well as seasoned veterans—everything they needed in a lighthearted mini manual. And Dan was in full agreement with the idea that each person in the company sit down with his three to five most important Trapeze Buddies, completing a win-win report card.

The intense ringing of the "hot line" on Dan's desk startled everyone in attendance. The focused trance had been broken. Excusing himself, Dan answered the phone.

"Great afternoon, Dan here."

The voice on the other end was filled with urgency. "Dan, this is Mary at the rehab center."

Dan immediately recognized her voice. They had worked closely together for the last four years, and he had developed immense respect and admiration for her vision, dedication and boundless energy in working with the patients. He quickly inquired, "Is everything okay, Mary?"

She went right to the point. "Dan, I hate to bother you, but I wouldn't do so if it wasn't of the utmost importance."

"Go on," encouraged the CEO.

"Dan, is there any way you can get down to the rehab center in the next ten to fifteen minutes? It's pretty important."

"Well, Mary," Dan began, evaluating his options before completing his answer, "I'm in the middle of a meeting right now. Is everything okay? Is everyone all right?"

"Yes," offered Mary, "but it would be best if you could be here in person. I hate to push, but could you make it down here, pronto?"

Dan knew Mary wouldn't request his presence unless it was extremely important. "I'll be there in 12 minutes."

Hanging up the phone, he grabbed his jacket and started his stopwatch in one fluid movement, informed the team of the pending emergency and instructed them to keep the process moving forward. He looked down at his stopwatch: 23 seconds flat!

Fortunately, the drive to the rehab center was a short six miles. Yet, despite the short distance, Dan's mind raced over the many possibilities of the urgent call. Was someone sick or injured? Perhaps a key staff member had announced his departure. Was everything alright with Byron? The six mile drive generated 6,000 thoughts, questions and concerns.

Whipping his car into the parking lot, Dan pushed the gear into park and headed for the front door. He glanced at his watch, nine minutes twelve seconds— he was right on target.

Dan's "forced march" slowed as he entered the lobby, performing his reconnaissance to determine a cause for the urgency while searching for Mary. Standing at the end of the hall, she waved for Dan to move quickly toward her. He picked up the pace. "Thank you for coming, Dan," Mary whispered. "It means a lot that you could be here."

Dan locked arms with Mary as she led him forward. "What's going on? What's happening here?" Mary put her fingers to her lips, signaling Dan to hold his questions. She nodded positively and whispered, "You'll find out in a moment."

The duo soon moved through double doors leading to a large, sun drenched recreation room. A crowd was huddled tightly around a common focal point. Dan couldn't tell what was happening or determine the object demanding such attention.

As they moved toward the group, the only sound to be heard was their four feet tapping a rhythm on the wood floor. Mary and Dan approached arm in arm as bodies parted to reveal their point of interest. Byron was sitting tall in his wheel chair with cautious optimism on his face and an intensity in his eye which Dan had not often seen. Byron looked up, smiled at the CEO, and nodded to his parents, who stepped away from their son.

What happened next can only be described as a miracle, a blessing from the full hand of God. Dan watched in amazement as Byron used his strong arms to push himself up out of the wheelchair into a standing position. He pressed against his chair, supported by his strong arms. Byron's trainer then handed the young man two walking canes that wrapped around the forearms of the determined lad.

Not a sound could be heard in the room. Breathing had come to a halt except for the labored breath of the center of attention, who established the support of the walking canes, checked his balance, and straightened his posture. Byron looked down at his feet, then up

The Trapeze Buddy Success Strategy

toward the heavens, and with the greatest of concentration, focus and effort moved his left foot six inches forward. He rested the weight of his body on his foot and then meticulously moved his right foot parallel with his left.

Hands of the observers went toward their mouths. Byron wobbled, straightened his strong frame, and moved his left foot forward another six inches. He had now walked an entire twelve inches on the strength of his own legs. The canes supported his balance, but he had clearly taken the steps on his own power. He had walked.

Sometimes silence says more than a thousand cheers. Who would dare spoil the magic of the moment? Byron's two feet moved forward twice more, beads of sweat pouring down his face. Byron bent over his canes and let out a loud, heartfelt "**YES!**"

"So this is what Mary wanted me to see," thought Dan as he choked back both a cheer and a tear. "I guess when it's time to take your first step, you don't wait; you go for it."

Suddenly the group exploded into applause. Each person present as a witness had a stake in the thirty-six inches covered in those three steps. For each person it was a labor of love, patience and hope. After

Byron signaled for his chair, he was quickly surrounded by his adoring fans.

Dan noticed circus star Alex, the giant of a man, attempting to hold back tears of excitement. Dan also watched Byron's two buddies, Scott and Tony, applauding from their wheel chairs, celebrating the victory of a good friend and soaking in the hope that this moment offered to them. Hugs, words of encouragement and tears of joy flowed nonstop.

Dan turned to Mary. "Thanks for pressing me to be here. You knew I wouldn't want to miss this monumental day."

Mary smiled, "I'm just glad I didn't have to spill the beans on the surprise or drag you over here under force."

It was finally Dan's turn to acknowledge the star of the moment. As he approached his good friend, emotion welled up in Dan's heart. He hugged his Trapeze Buddy with an embrace that told the entire story. It had been a long road of sweat, tears and some discouraging moments, but three giant steps made it all worthwhile. They had done it; Byron had walked.

Gazing at Dan with gratitude, Byron was the first to break the silence. "The other day we were talking about first steps. You took one with the Trapeze Buddy project at your company last night. I took one today. Only difference is that I had to put in all the hard work before taking the first step. You have to take the first step, then put in the hard work."

Dan was again stunned by Byron's insight. But then the young man added his customary zinger, "And I'll bet my steps have been faster and further than yours!"

Dan thumped Byron lovingly on the head. Byron was right. They had both taken giant strides.

Epilogue

Fast forward two years...

Executive Assistant, Nathalie, retired from BoMar after the stock options made her a multi-millionaire. She and her husband have joined the circus and are touring the country as part of a Flying Trapeze act.

Darrell, the Limo Driver, bought the limo company he had been working for. He fired the boss and the pathetic presenter who conducted his new hire orientation, then sold the company for a big profit. He plays golf at least two times a week and volunteers at the Spinal Cord Rehab Center. He has two dogs.

Barb Moss still works at BoMar. In fact, she's the new CEO, hand picked and mentored by Dan. She races cars on the weekends and has a new tattoo.

Flying Trapeze Artist, Alex, gave up the circus and is now putting on Executive Trapeze Programs with WOW! Performance Coaching across the country. He still volunteers with kids and now runs marathons, raising money for leukemia research.

Tom Murphy, Former Head of HR at BoMar, is serving a prison term for embezzlement from his daughter's elementary school PTA fund. Seems he didn't CYB quite well enough.

Byron, our paraplegic hero, has his driver's license and is a huge hit with the ladies. Byron is a motivational speaker, working with kids and physically challenged adults. Each day he practices on his walking skills, which are slowly progressing. He now uses one walking cane for support. He owns a Labrador retriever.

Dan, the Flying CEO, sold his stake in BoMar, put Barb in his place as CEO and now lives in a mountain top retreat when he's not on the pro golf circuit. His writings and speeches have touched millions of lives on virtually every continent—he is a Trapeze Buddy personified. Dan has a passion for Dixieland Jazz music, so he is learning to play the clarinet.

Acknowledgements

To move a book from concept to finished product requires a team effort. Countless hands and eyes have touched and reviewed the manuscript. Numerous conversations have influenced the direction of the Trapeze Buddy metaphor. Thousands of seminar and conference participants have validated the real-world application to their business life.

My heartfelt "Thanks" is extended to all who have touched this work in their unique way.

I want to begin formal acknowledgements by publicly thanking my right arm and master marketing guru, Beth Boyd, for her relentless pursuit to get this book out of my head and onto paper. She has worked countless hours reading, reviewing, editing and typing as well as pulling together all the pieces to move this from concept to a real book. Thanks for your persistence, encouragement and kick in the back end!

Many friends and colleagues invested their own time in the peer review process offering ideas, plenty of red ink, insights and enhancements to add life to the project. My thanks to Bob Googe, George Jackson, Cinda Daly, Jerry Fritz, Greg Cortopassi, Lou Webber, Don Nelson, Jeanne Imbrogno, Mark Sanborn, Sherrie

Rosenberger, Malcolm Franks, Tom Hinton, Jack Simpson, Dad Rosenberger and Sally Gavin.

Dr. Jim DeSaegher was awesome as the lead editor. Your insights and mastery are evident on every page. You've forgotten more than I'll ever know about writing, editing and proper sentence structure. A most sincere Thanks!

Several amazing Tuesday morning, lakeside devotions with Brad Sousa helped move me forward. This book is evidence of moving beyond fear and operating from a position of trust. Thanks, Brad!

Finally, I've been told the key to being a good author is to have a supportive family. I have the best—a wife, Sherrie, who believes in me and a son, Mikael, who is a world class encourager! The perfect Trapeze Buddies!

About the Author

Mark Rosenberger is the Founder and Director of WOW! Performance Coaching, Inc.

As a professional speaker and consultant, Mark shares ideas, concepts and strategies with corporations, associations and professional groups in Canada, the United States, Mexico and South America, blending his messages with passion, humor and contagious enthusiasm.

His extensive background provides an unparalleled perspective. His experience includes education, sales and sales management, senior management, entrepreneur, consultant, innovator, author, husband, father, and marathon runner helping raise money for Leukemia research.

Equally important to Mark's experience are his accomplishments and the results clients report from his work. He has created and designed numerous training programs currently used in schools and corporations across America.

Client results include:
- **Reduction of employee turnover by 54%; increase in tips by more than 30%**
- **Doubling Repeat and Referral business**
- **More fun on the job and increased innovation**

He is the author/co-author of three books and dozens of articles focusing on customer service, teamwork and performance enhancement issues. You can find Mark's articles and more at **www.WowCoaching.com**.

Mark lives with his wife, Sherrie, son, Mikael, and their chocolate Labrador retrievers, George and Tucker, in San Diego, California.

A Great Opportunity to Make a Difference…

Since 2000, I've had the privilege of running (and completing) marathons on behalf of the Leukemia & Lymphoma Society.

My purpose is to raise awareness of these blood related cancers and contribute money through donations to researching a cure.

You may not know, but Leukemia is the number one killer of children under the age of 14 and twice as many adults suffer from this disease.

If you know of someone directly or indirectly who has experienced either Leukemia or Lymphoma, we'd like to make them an "Honored Teammate." We'll wear a ribbon and run the 26.2 miles on their behalf. Last year I wore 15 ribbons—some for survivors, some in various stages of treatment and several in memory of loved ones.

The Society is a **GREAT** place to get involved if you're looking for an opportunity to make a difference. Donations of time and money are needed. I'm proud to say that 75% of all funds raised went directly toward researching a cure! Pretty impressive!

For more information visit their website at: www.Leukemia.org

Thanks for making a difference!

Order More Trapeze Buddy Books and Tapes:

The Book—The Trapeze Buddy Success Strategy:
A New Way to Create Trust, Support and Teamwork in Your Business
Book—US$17.95

The Tape Series—Trapeze Buddies:
How to be Caught More and Dropped Less by the People You Count on Most
Four Audio Tape Series & Workbook—US$79.95

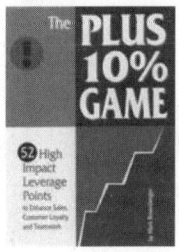

The PLUS 10% Game:
52 High Impact Leverage Points to Enhance Sales, Customer Service and Teamwork
Book—US$19.95

TO ORDER:
1-888-WOW-YOU2 (1-888-969-9682)
or visit: www.TrapezeBuddy.com
or fax: 1-858-578-7065
Visa, MasterCard, American Express, Discover, checks or small unmarked bills

Bring the TRAPEZE BUDDY™ Message to your Company or Organization:

- On-site training and consulting services
- Customized workshops and keynote speeches
- Learning tools, reinforcement ideas, success strategies

Visit our website at:
WWW.TRAPEZEBUDDY.COM
or call direct **1-858-578-7900**

WOW! *Performance Coaching, Inc.*
info@wowcoaching.com
1-858-578-7900